Chase Two Horses

proverbs and sayings
for an everyday spirituality

Charles R. Ringma

PiQUANT
editions

Contents

Preface

One of my favourite proverbs is: the one "who rides the tiger is afraid to dismount."[1] The basic meaning of this Chinese proverb is that once a difficult project is undertaken or a challenging course of action is set in motion, the best way forward is to see it through to the end. The implication in this proverb is that to give up partway or to dismount may result in harm.

One can easily draw much more from this proverb. To some extent, proverbs—like metaphors—are layered with meanings. They are small packages of practical wisdom.

I was brought up in an extended family in Holland and in a culture where proverbs were often used as a way of encouragement or correction. Having lived in different countries, I have come to see how proverbs are evident in so many cultures. What a rich resource for our globalised world!

The seed for this book was planted by my mother-in-law, Harmina Dijk-Pesman, who one day, in her late-eighties, handed me a little red book filled with the proverbs she remembered and sought to live by. So when I quote from this, it will be Oma's[2] handwritten "Little Red Book."[3] Around the same time, my beloved aunt in the Netherlands, Tante Riek de Jong, sent me an anthology of Dutch proverbs, thereby adding fuel to the fire.[4] There had to be a message in this somewhere!

When a proverb in English has its source in another language, I will attempt to reference that. And when a far more evocative proverb in another language has an English equivalent, the English version will appear in the proverb index. For example, the German proverb, "mit der Tür ins Haus fallen,"[5] literally means "to fall into the house with the door." But its meaning has to do with jumping into a matter without proper warning and preparation. The English meaning, "to butt at once into the thick of the matter,"[6] is a translation that would appear in the index. The topical index will identify the way in which I have used the proverb for a philosophical, theological, or ethical reflection.

There are a number of thanks in order. First of all, the members of our writers group, who are affectionately called the "holy" scribblers: Terry Gatfield, Jill Manton, Chris Brown, Irene Alexander, John Steward, and Sarah Nicholls have had a daily immersion in these proverbs during our writer's retreats. They are still smiling!

Karen Hollenbeck-Wuest has cast her careful and loving eye over this manuscript, and Pieter Kwant, my literary agent, has once again taking this project in hand. Thank you, each one!

Charles Ringma
Brisbane, Australia, 2018

Introduction

Growing up in the historic Friesian town of Franeker in Northern Holland with aunts, uncles, and grandparents nearby—in fact, within walking distance—I can remember hearing proverbs quoted to make a particular succinct point. These proverbs usually had a moral message and encouraged good behaviour.

The proverb I remember the best was: "de laatste loodjes wegen het zwaarst."[7] Roughly translated, this means that the last part of a task is often the hardest to complete. The English equivalent is: "the last mile is the longest."[8]

This proverb was often quoted to me because, as a young boy, I had the tendency to move too quickly from one thing to another and did not always finish the task at hand. I suppose I got bored too quickly. Clearly my grandparents were trying to instil the quality of perseverance in me. They may have succeeded?

In our present-day conversations, we tend not to hear such proverbs in our homes, our relationships with our friends, or the workplace. Nor is contemporary literature replete with proverbs. We seem to think that these proverbs are far too archaic and moralistic.

It is true that many of the Western proverbs came into use in a world where tradition, family, and work values were shaped by both Greek philosophical and general Christian values, and proverbs from other cultures often reflected older traditions and values.

But with the collapse of Christendom in the West and our globalised twenty-first century world with its largely post-modern values, it no longer seems appropriate to pass on these words of lived wisdom. In our hyper-individualistic society, we are encouraged to make our way, find our own path, and create our own self-identity. Moreover, the idea of being mentored in ways of looking at the world and living out certain established values seems far too archaic for many of us. Such teaching and values may be okay for monks, but not for us urban dwellers—who are no longer "dwellers," but ever on the move. The "nomads" of late modernity certainly don't need a settled wisdom, but only the thrill of new places and experiences.

However, let me suggest that there are several reasons for recovering the use of these proverbs and sayings.

First and foremost, it is exhausting to grow up in a world where everything needs to be self-discovered and nothing is passed on. The world of "me" as a self-enclosed entity is a very narrow world, indeed. Surely, an openness to assimilation and integration from others helps us to forge an enhanced and enlarged self.

Second, we need ground under our feet if we truly wish to fly. We need a broad ethic as a framework for our being and acting in the world. With the ongoing negativity that so many people have for religious institutions, the wisdom of these proverbs and sayings may provide a rich resource for living well and helping us to discern pitfalls and dead-end streets. Of course, this wisdom needs to be voluntarily embraced, and we can only live it well when word becomes deed.

Third, recovering the wisdom of these proverbs may help us begin to shape what is so blatantly lacking in our present world—a sense of commonality. As a sociologically fragmented and culturally and ethically diverse people, we have lost much of the glue that helps us to live in ways that create community and make life whole. While drawn from many different cultures and over several thousand years, the proverbs in these pages reflect a practical wisdom that can serve us well.

Rather than simply repeating a particular proverb, my aim in this book is to interact with and unpack each proverb by offering an extended philosophical, theological, spiritual, and ethical reflection. My hope is that this reflection will help make these proverbs more accessible and relevant for our time.

intuitive powers. After all, science and the imagination are not opposed to each other.

The Chinese proverb, "water thirty-three feet deep is easily measured, but a person's thoughts are hard to fathom,"[12] may be helpful at this point. In other words, there are things we can easily measure, which, by way of extension, we can easily make or control. But there is also much that we don't know, including the creative groaning within society and the inner musings of the human being for good or ill.

Not only are our inner thoughts a mystery to others, but they are also often a mystery to ourselves. Much of our inner life is a curious amalgam of our biology, personal upbringing, life circumstances, and cultural conditioning, along with our fears, complexes, hopes, and dreams. Our archetypical connections with our forebears add a further layer of mystery to this complex mix.

Moreover, we are shaped by ideological and religious configurations. Regarding the latter dimension, if the gods or spirits are involved in our inner musings and imaginations, then the realm of mystery opens even further—perhaps into an abyss.

The complexity of our inner lives does not invite us into a violent exorcism or reductionism, where we seek to make certain melody lines dominant and reduce others to a simplistic or clichéd formula. But rather, we engage in a multi-level attentiveness. This approximates the prophetic imagination of the Old Testament, where the prophets, who were persons of prayer and socio-political insight, provided a profound critique of the misuse of power in their culture and cast a vision of renewal for the future.

Thus we need to think hard about things and engage our world critically, but we must also dream and pray. Though much will remain hidden from our sight, we journey forward in faith.

BEYOND STRUCTURES

a spirituality of personalism

No one knows where the shoe pinches as well as the one who wears it.

In the twentieth century, industrial progress and its related urbanisation led many to fear that people would end up as cogs in the machine and as vague spectres in a mass society.

Our post-industrial world, despite all its promises, has not diminished these fears. In our predominately urban surveillance society, we feel subjected to the larger economic and global forces of our world. With the robotization of the workplace and other dimensions of life, we feel our smallness and irrelevance. Our global neo-liberal society has invaded us to the point where we seem to be losing ourselves. Common causes that erode individual significance is ultimately destructive and unsustainable.

Yet seeking only inward significance hardly allays our fears, since the all-pervasive world continues to shape our inner-scape. While the human quest for freedom can be cast in terms of self-preoccupation and what we have been liberated *from*, sustainable freedom must be cast in terms of freedom *for*—for the other, for responsibility, for well-being, for the common good.

Thus rather than escaping into an isolationist individualism, we need to be actively involved in creating communities that enhance the common good, but that are also concerned with individual well-being. We may need to call these "communities of resistance."

The well-known German proverb, "jeder weiss am besten, wo ihn Schuh drückt," or "no one knows where the shoe pinches as well as the one who wears it,"[13] is a helpful reminder of this tension between individualism and communalism.

This saying does not suggest that our life is forged only in the good things that we share and have in common. Rather, it is also shaped in the places where we are being hindered, pressed down, and hemmed in, where we are being silenced or shut down, where we are hurting.

We are increasingly pressed down and hemmed in by the corporatization of life. This is even happening in Christian institutions and in the church, which should be spaces for radical egalitarianism through the redemptive work of Christ, levelling us all as brothers and sisters through grace.

The more top-down and dictatorial our institutions become, the more people will begin to complain of hurting feet. Hurting feet are not ideal for walking a common journey. They may well become the genesis for protest. Thus a fracturing will occur, and the seeming strength of those in power may weaken.

Shoes need to fit, which means that many of our institutions and places of work need to find a better balance between group identity and individual well-being.

An ill-fitting shoe is like a canary in a coal mine. We best listen to its warning call before the canary is dead.

<u>6</u>

SEEING AGAIN

the silent gift of time

Good water even if made murky will become clear again
after the dirt has settled.

In the midst of life, when we are in full stride, things can suddenly go horribly wrong. The wheels fall off the cart, so to speak—an illness, perhaps, or a job loss. Whatever the jolt may be, the brutal reality is that life is not determined simply by our choices, planning, or control. Life is much bigger, and anything can come our way. Thus we live with a fundamental vulnerability, which can generate insecurity and fear within us.

But even more corrosive than an external crisis is the slow and often imperceptible erosion of our well-being and values. Even while everything is going well in our personal lives and our vocational settings, we can lose our way. The waters can become muddied.

The Filipino proverb, "good water even if made murky will become clear after the dirt has settled,"[14] expresses hope in the midst of this eventuality.

In the midst of a crisis or in the process of slow erosion, we can become reactionary and blind, quick to blame someone else and feel sorry for ourselves. In these circumstances, while it may be necessary to take some sort of remedial action, it may also be appropriate to give ourselves the gift of time. Sometimes reflection is more helpful than immediate—and often reactive—action.

In our garden, we have half of a wooden wine barrel that functions as a fish pond. Due to rapid evaporation in the often brutal Queensland sun, I have to pour several buckets of water into the barrel to top it up once a week. This stirs up the slush at the bottom, and for several days, the pond is murky. But then it settles again, and I see the fish.

So it is with life. Things can become murky and confused. While reaction always lies close at hand, we may need to give ourselves the gift of time to reflect, think, meditate, and pray. We need this time both during a crisis and when things are going seemingly well—perhaps even more when things are going well!

Yet we are often not generous with ourselves, and this reflects the driven nature of our lives and the all-too-invasive nature of contemporary culture.

While we may think that monks live an irrelevant lifestyle, they can teach us about the need to be quiet and contemplative, to create better rhythms of engagement and disengagement, and to let murkiness and confusion settle by giving them the gift of time.

The gift of time allows our more immediate thoughts, responses, and reactions to fade, which may give space for the more lasting and helpful responses to swim into view.

Let the murky water in your pond settle so you can see clearly!

OPENNESS

a spirituality of vulnerability

Shared sorrow is half the grief.

In a much earlier age, we were defined by family solidarity, local community, and communal identity. We were usually known as the son or daughter of the *burgher* of the town, and even our grandparents shaped our identity.

But this age has long slipped through our fingers, and our contemporary world is made up of fragile and often dysfunctional families, suspicion and isolation, high mobility, and the burdensome task of perpetually creating a "new" identity.

In this world of movement, pragmatism, personal makeover, and reinvention, we are identified by a series of images on a fast-moving screen. Yet despite our connectivity through images, we suffer from an existential loneliness and an unidentifiable angst. Not even our therapeutic culture, with its dependence on the psychiatrist couch and drug use, provides a sustainable basis for our fragmentary existence.

In seeking to overcome and transcend the blight of the philosophy and practical outworking of the mantra of the autonomous self, neither our work environment—with its increasing flexibility and unreliability— nor our recreational activities, nor our well-being programs, are sufficient. These are all personal choices and merely reinforce the self-determining self.

We need to find new ways of connectedness that join us with something greater than ourselves. Rather than a constant "projected" self, we need to grow into an enhanced self through solidarity with others.

One surprising way this can occur is through the connectedness that erupts when tragedy strikes a city or community. Fires, floods, and other disasters can draw people together in amazing ways.

The Dutch proverb, "gedeelde smart is halve smart,"[15] or shared sorrow is half the grief, points us in this direction.

Along with communal tragedies, shared individual struggles can draw people together and evoke a repository of responses in people's hearts. Our competitive successes are not the glue that binds us together. Rather, difficulty, loss, grief, and shared suffering forge communities of solidarity and care.

Yet it can be challenging to find ways to make the unusual more normative. Communal solidarity that is forged through tragedy so quickly dissipates, and soon it is back "to business as usual."

We can move forward by forging friendships of openness and vulnerability and also by remaining in solidarity with the suffering that continues in so many parts of our world—including our own backyard.

Though ability may create heroes, and success may invite admiration, and our projected images of ourselves may create envy, openness and vulnerability build community.

INTENTIONALITY

putting things to their proper use

From the same flower the bee makes honey,
but the spider makes venom.

There are very basic ways in which we can view the world and our fellow human beings. One way is to see everything as inherently good. The opposite is to perceive everything as somehow evil. Clearly, there are other ways to think about others and our world.

The basic Christian view is that everything is good because a benevolent God created all in love. But what God made has become marred by human folly and wrongdoing. Yet this is not the end of the story, for the Creator God set in motion the work of redemption and is seeking to restore all things.

Such a perspective implies that our world is conflicted. In a good world, evil is present, but so is the work of healing and restoration. We can cooperate with one or the other. We can enhance the good and resist what is evil, although this is far easier said than done. Even though a fundamental goodness marks us, so do our stupidities—even when the grace of God is at work in our lives and world.

was singularly uninspiring, and so I began to notice what the people around me were doing.

Next to me, a young medical student was attempting to attend to a fat textbook on gynaecology. But every four to five minutes, he turned to his mobile phone to check Facebook and Instagram. As time went on, I began to feel sorry for him. He was wasting so much time, possibly to hear from someone that he was valued.

And so it is. We cry that we are time poor, but we spend hours communicating our banalities. What dreariness!

The warning against burning a candle to find a flea is a wake-up call for the modern world. So much time and energy—not to mention the expense of our technological devices—for so little gain!

While not decrying the value of modern technology—just as we would not decry the value of a candle in an older world—our challenge is to put what we have to good use. We should not fritter our lives away. And there is no need to spend much time and energy on what is banal and irrelevant. We are here for more purposeful things.

Use a candle to shed light on someone's pathway, or to read a challenging book, rather than to catch a flea!

11

BLINDNESS

the challenging art of seeing

People are blind in their own cause.

The English language is replete with proverbs about blindness. Some are particularly telling: "a pebble and a diamond are alike to a blind person," or "a blind person will not thank you for a looking glass." But here I will focus on: "people are blind in their own cause."[19]

This proverb is timely and relevant as we experience the "culture wars" of the twenty-first century. It is even more challenging as we seek to come to terms with our globalised world and our multicultural societies.

For instance, those who are secularised find it bizarre that there are people who not only believe in God, but who take the Bible seriously and seek to live by its precepts. Others find it preposterous that there are ethnic groups in their societies that practice female genital mutilation. On and on, one group is appalled by the blindness and stupidity of the other. This is further complicated by the fact that there are people in the world today who live by premodern, modern, postmodern, and now post-postmodern values.

As we try to live in a world with such a kaleidoscope of beliefs and values, we are not only confused and bewildered, but we wonder whether we are all blind. To put that somewhat differently, maybe the way toward a better and more peaceful world is to stop believing in anything. But this does not get us very far. To believe in nothing is still a belief system.

Is there another way? Since we are meaning-making and social creatures, systems of belief, worship, doctrine, and values will inevitably be practised and will continue to emerge in new configurations. The challenge for those within such systems is to avoid making them self-referential silos.

Thus we remain committed to our beliefs, but we are radically open to the other. In trying to live this out, the core concept of loving our neighbour is a window of opportunity.

Such love calls for openness, respect, and care for the other, as well as dialogue and the interchange of ideas and values. This love invites us not only to face our own biases and misunderstandings about the other, but also to attempt to understand our own traditions and values more carefully. This is necessary, because every ideological or religious system over time accrues barnacles that need to be scraped away.

Is this possible? Social philosophers such as Jürgen Habermas call us to communicative competence. Others call us to interfaith dialogue. Others call us to practice the general values of fairness, justice, and freedom.

But however we move forward, we must not remain blind in our silos.

BETRAYAL

healing relational conflict

A double-crossing friend knows more what harms you.

As social creatures, our relationships are intrinsic to who we are, but it does not take long to discover the precarious nature of relationships. Many people are wounded during their childhood years by unhealthy family dynamics. Once we have become more self-determining and assume that we can manage our own adult relationships much better, we soon discover that this, too, is a rocky road.

We can shrug off many of the relational conflicts that we experience in daily life—particularly when the relationships are not that close or meaningful.

But other relational difficulties almost undo us. The Arabic proverb, "a double-crossing friend knows more what harms you,"[20] woefully reflects this. Such experiences leave us feeling naked and exposed.

The more we share with another person, the more that person knows and understands us, the more they can hurt us.

Most of us have experienced this in some form or other. We know something of the beauty of a deep relationship and friendship, and we have sadly had to live with its painful undoing. This pain goes on when reconciliation, after many attempts, does not seem possible.

At this point, we need to consider what can be done to mitigate this painful loss. Denying our hurt will not help us. Simply blaming a former friend will only give us temporary relief. We need to find a way forward.

A starting point is to grieve our loss by reflecting, over days and weeks, on what was good in the friendship. We may journal about this or find other symbolic ways to revisit what was special and life-giving in the relationship. This can be an unhurried process, particularly as we reflect on what the friendship has added to our life.

A second move is to reflect on the ways we have failed our former friend—without making a dark and self-condemning archaeological expedition into our own inner being. Acknowledging these failures to ourselves can be a healing process.

A third move is to hold in our heart the torch of forgiveness towards our former friend. This light can keep self-pity and anger at bay. It can also open us to what may yet happen. Most importantly, it can prevent us from closing down on other friendships.

When a friend wounds us, we have to engage in healing practices.

APPEARANCES

beyond an outward image

Not all chefs carry their special knives.

We are living in a time when everyone seems to want to be famous by posting pictures in the public arena. So much of our contemporary life is about projecting the right image. In fact, some think that life is *only* about image.

The Dutch proverb, "het zijn niet allen koks die lange messen dragen," or "not all chefs carry their special knives," has a long history with many variants. Following are just a few: "not all Doctors [Professors] wear their red bonnets"; "not all huntsmen blow their horns"; and "not all religious go happily to church."[21]

The point of these proverbs is that we should not lock our perception of a person into certain appearances and behaviours, because there is much more to a person than image, and there are always exceptions to any rule.

More contemporary sayings might be: not every politician only serves his or her party; not every rich person drives a Lamborghini.

While stereotypical behaviours make social life more predictable, judging and making assumptions about others by outward appearance overlooks human diversity.

Most striking to me are the women and men who have deliberately sought to live beyond stereotypes.

I think of one of my highly intelligent friends who worked at a railway siding and read philosophy and poetry to his workmates during the lunch hour. I know an Asian businessman who drove an ordinary fifteen-year-old car and spent much of his time voluntarily mentoring young entrepreneurs. There was a Benedictine Abbott who donned his gum boots and overalls to muck out the pig sty each afternoon. The point here is that social conventions are helpful, but they don't—and can't—tell the whole story.

To put this more pointedly, an academic gown does not make a person a good lecturer, and someone with the trappings of the rich is not necessarily a wise or nice person.

This invites us to look at people in terms of their character and virtues, rather than their status and appearance. Our most critical concerns should be people's commitment to fairness, justice, generosity, and the common good.

Beyond our public image, which is a chimera of smoke and mirrors, is a real "world" that reveals who we are when no one is watching and when we are not wearing our gowns.

RESTORATION

giving back what we have taken

The frog does not drink up the pond in which it lives.

There was a time, not so many decades ago, when we thought that the earth's resources were limitless and that we could continue to exploit them as much as we could. Thankfully, we no longer think that way. We now live with a much greater sense of the fragility of our world and our need to care for it. But whether we do that well at a personal or national level remains a pressing and open question.

The American Native proverb, "the frog does not drink up the pond in which it lives,"[22] helps us to think more about this issue.

While our existence is far more demanding than for the frog, and our population growth continues, we do need to grasp that life has a reciprocal movement and is about give and take. We need to give back, and this needs to occur in every sphere of life—family, business, society, and nature.

At certain points in our life cycle, we may need to receive more than we are able to give. This may be regarded as the nurturing phase or the training phase. But there comes a time when we are expected to give as well. The movement from power *for* someone (nutrition) to power *with* someone (mutuality) is the movement to growth and greater responsibility. One matures in order to give.

This is also true regarding our relationship with the earth. We can and need to give back. The earth sustains us. We owe it our very life. There is something sacred about its giving power, and its creative and renewing powers are awesome. But the earth and its capacities are not limitless.

The earth has become wounded and needs healing and restoration. Our stewardship has been poor. We have exploited the earth and given little back. We have been greedy and ungrateful.

Finally, we are realising that the wounded earth is reacting to our negligence. The earth is responding, and we are suffering.

While we need to do all we can at a personal level to live more simply and carefully, our efforts can never restore what we have so blatantly abused. Care for the planet earth needs to be embraced more fully as a national and global agenda, particularly when crude isolationism is being championed in many parts of the world, and scepticism regarding the earth's vulnerability is trumpeted everywhere.

The mantra of short-term economic gain needs to be challenged by the logic of long-term sustainability. We need to be concerned about the whole—not only our puny and feeble patches. Commonwealth and common sustainability are inter-related notions.

As the pond diminishes, the frog's existence comes under threat. It's high time to bring the pond back to an earlier pristine condition.

15

LOVE'S FIRE

the disruptive ways of love

Love laughs at locksmiths.

In an often dreary world, love brings colour and hope—a great surprise that springs from the unknown places of the human heart. Once love rises, there are no limits to where it might take us.

While love may stir as a faint whisper or gentle breeze, it more often envelops us in a cloud that may blind us at first, but then reorients us. Love has a power that unsettles us and guides us onto new pathways.

When we experience love's initial ways, we know that we are not in control, but are swept up, overwhelmed. The heart, once awakened, leaps over its banks like a raging river, carrying along everything in its path.

The nineteenth-century English proverb, "love laughs at locksmiths,"[23] opens up playful reflections that can take us in many directions.

Most basically, we cannot dam the force of love within our lives—no matter how much we may try! Though the mind may try to reason with love, it is an irrational force that disdains logic and takes risks, bringing us into unfamiliar territory and interrupting our prosaic existence.

More complexly, when self-giving love flows to others without seeking to control them, it can break down barriers. Its winsome ways can crack the walls of resistance and indifference.

But all around us are gainsayers who fear love's ways and gravitate towards predictability and safety, the routines of life rather than the strange ways of love.

It is not particularly strange to fall in love with another person, for that is basic to the human condition, but it is somewhat strange to fall in love with art, music, or a social or political cause. And in our rather sceptical contemporary world, it is even stranger to fall in love with a spiritual being or to say that we love God above all else.

Yet, some may love God so much that they live the rest of their lives in a monastic community, devoting themselves to a life of prayer, and there are others who serve God by caring for those who are most vulnerable and destitute.

While the initial fires of love need to be forged into long-term habits and commitments, that initial eruption of love can inspire and sustain us when all is sorely tried and tested. Then love's resilient power becomes all the stronger.

May love continue its disruptive ways in our world, which is so full of predictability!

FRUITFUL RESISTANCE

a spirituality of discernment

To kick against the pricks.

Many people happily live their lives believing that everything that happens in society is benign and that those in positions of power—whether political, business, or social—work for the common good. These people basically accept everything and question nothing.

At the other end of the spectrum are those who question and suspect everything. Marked by this hermeneutics of suspicion, they assume that everyone in power misuses their position.

Clearly, the reality lies somewhere in between. Certainly not everyone in power is self-serving, and not every agent for radical change is discerning and well-motivated.

Knowing what to accept gratefully and what to resist calls for careful discernment. It is difficult to know when a cause is good or hopeless. But it may also be true that no cause is hopeless, even when we make no headway and the hoped-for outcomes fade into the distant horizon.

The well-known proverb, "to kick against the pricks"—and its French equivalent, "regimber contre l'éperon"—is based on Saul's visionary encounter with the risen Christ (Acts 9:4–5). The proverb is interpreted by the Dutch specialist F. A. Stoett to mean, "vruchteloze tegenstand bieden,"[24] which literally means "to give fruitless resistance." In other words, it is continuing to fight in a hopeless cause and thus do damage to ourselves. A similar expression is, "stop hitting your head against the wall."

Saul's aim was to persecute everyone who believed in this new Messiah and thus stop early Christianity in its tracks. His visionary experience caused him to see this as a wrong cause.

If we embrace a wrong cause, somewhere in the endeavour, we will hopefully come to see the light. But when the cause is good, do we press on—even when it seems hopeless? And do we continue even at great cost to ourselves? Is it okay to be "bloodied" in a just cause?

The clear answer is, "yes," so long as we are shedding our own blood and not the blood of those we oppose. It is also appropriate to continue working for a good cause even when there is no progress at all.

Together with my friends, I worked for twenty years in drug prevention and rehabilitation while the problem only got worse. And I have been involved in other causes with refugees where, to date, no progress has been made.

Dietrich Bonhoeffer fought a lost cause in opposing Hitler and lost his life. But was this a lost cause? Indeed, not. To "stop kicking against pricks" is to give up on a bad cause, but if the cause is good, the challenge is to continue against all odds—both for our own sense of integrity and as a witness to future generations. To be "bloodied" for a good cause, even when we fail, is the seed for a new tomorrow.

EFFECTUAL RESISTANCE

a spirituality of subversion

To put a stick in the wheel.

We live in world where there is an ever-greater collusion between powerful forces in society and an undermining of the separation of powers. We see this in multinational corporations that exercise excessive influence over scientific, military, and economic powers.

In such a world, citizens feel increasingly powerless, and forms of protest can seem to be ineffectual. Just ask those who have protested against various forms of the misuse of power in their country! In these circumstances it is so easy to give up. To resist seems to be a useless endeavour.

But to give up on our human agency diminishes both our humanity and the wider community. The Dutch proverb, "een spaak in het wiel steken,"[25] challenges us in this regard. Roughly translated, this means "to put a stick in the wheel," which practically means to deliberately—through some decisive action—attempt to derail a plan or certain activity.

This saying has been applied to the life of the German theologian and martyr Dietrich Bonhoeffer. In his resistance to Nazi ideology, Bonhoeffer eventually joined the *Abwehr*—the counterintelligence organisation consisting of senior members of the military along with certain civilian advisors. Initially unknown to Hitler, this organisation was highly critical of the government and sought ways to remove Hitler from power.

Bonhoeffer joined the *Abwehr* to make contact with Christian leaders in overseas countries in order to gain support for the resistance to Hitler.

He made this move in the light of an ethical dilemma that he had posed to himself. Simply put, he raised the following question: if a madman is behind the steering wheel of a car, which has left the road and is driving on a footpath and running over people, is the ethical task to pick up the maimed and killed victims, or should one wrest the wheel out of the hand of the driver? Bonhoeffer concluded that one should stop the madman.

In Bonhoeffer's case, this involved being implicated in the use of violence to remove Hitler, which eventually cost him his life. Gandhi and Martin Luther King Jr., on the other hand, attempted to put a stick in the wheel through nonviolent protests.

Whatever approach we may use, being a stick in the wheel calls for creativity and a careful analysis about how to act. Most importantly, it calls for a willingness to suffer as we put our very life on the line.

ACCEPTING OUR GIFTEDNESS

a spirituality of grateful embrace

Not every flower can be a rose.

Life in the Western world as well as in many other cultures tends to be highly competitive.

Despite the framework of democracy, all sorts of hierarchies are evident: abled and disabled, male and female, smart and dumb, citizen and refugee. The list goes on and on, including one's professional status, ethnicity, and nationality.

Our culture assigns values to where we are situated in these distinctions, and we are economically rewarded for being higher up the "ladder." Some may even have the grossly misplaced idea that certain people are better morally because of their vocation or educational prowess.

This kind of thinking should be seriously challenged, as it can lead to all sorts of relational distortions and existential angst.

The Dutch proverb, "niet elke bloem kan een roos zijn,"[26] or "not every flower can be a rose," opens this topic for further reflection.

Just as the rose should not be regarded as the most beautiful flower—for what of the orchid?—so it follows that a film star need not be the most admired person. Nor should an academic be held in higher regard than a farmer.

This proverb implies that we should resist the human hierarchies that we have created and avoid falling into the trap of comparing ourselves with others.

This, of course, is easier said than done. Each society weaves powerful webs that place greater value on certain people, professions, and possessions.

To be able to live in the knowledge, acceptance, and joy of one's own giftedness—including what one is not and what one does not have—requires a countercultural spirituality. This means that we must gain our core values from somewhere besides society's pervasive propaganda.

This suggests the possibility that we can be in the world in a different way. We can live according to deeper spiritual values rather than be shaped by consumerism. We can be more communal rather than merely individualistic. We can be more reflective rather than simply pragmatic. We can be more peaceful rather than aggressive. The possibilities are endless.

But living more authentically in terms of who I am will make the world a more colourful place. A dull conformism does not make for a full life. To be clear, saying "yes" to who I am does *not* mean that I say "no" to the common good. In fact, the more I am truly myself, the greater my possible contribution will be.

MENDING

a spirituality of restoration

*It is better to fix what you have, than wait to get
what you don't have.*

Ours is an age where the mantra is "to move on." If things don't work, try
something else. If relationships break down, create new ones. If difficulties
come your way, move around them.

There are many factors in our social landscape that shape this kind
of thinking. One, is our throwaway culture. We don't fix things. We just
buy something new. Secondly, we are constantly sold the line that "there
may be something better." So rather than working at the possibility of
restoration, we look for a better job or partner. Thirdly, we live in a global
world that is "on the move." In many urban settings, up to 50 percent of
a neighbourhood moves elsewhere every four to five years. Thus, we are
always looking for something better elsewhere.

A well-known Arabic proverb points us in another direction: "it is
better to fix what you have, than wait to get what you don't have."[27]

This does not suggest that everything can be fixed, but we do need to try to restore things more than we do. For to restore something is not to make it exactly the same, but to bring newness to what was.

For example, when we seek to restore a broken relationship through the practices of forgiveness, restitution, and reconciliation, we do not bring the relationship back to the way it was before the breakdown. This is not possible, because the relationship has gone through the rugged journey of pain and disappointment. A certain kind of "death" has occurred. Thus repairing or mending the relationship involves a journey through "death" to "new life."

This movement is intrinsic to life itself. Our bodies are inherently restorative. To say, "I am sorry, please forgive me," is part of the relational glue in our lives. Moreover, God moves towards wayward humanity through restoration rather than condemnation or rejection.

In describing God's healing and restorative activity for humanity, feminist theologians use the term "mending" rather than the language of "liberation." This beautiful image emphasises that restoration is never an act of force or violence, but one of gentle care.

The image of mending brings us back to an older world—a grandmother in front of the fire mending holes in woollen socks. Though this may seem sentimental, it is powerfully symbolic. What was broken through the vicissitudes of life need not be discarded, but can be carefully taken up and mended.

Rather than living by the mantra, "move on," let us write a new melody line to "pick up and take care" of that which does not need to be discarded.

CONSTRAINTS

a spirituality of sober realism

The one who swallows 'udala' (apple) seed must consider the size of one's anus.

In our younger days, we may have thought that we could do everything, and we may have even thought that we could do something significant in our world. Yet the irresistible march of time and the sobering realities of life soon dampen our hopes and dreams.

Having thus been "bloodied" by the difficulties that have come our way, we have to find another way to position ourselves in the world. Some, of course, simply give up. "Life sucks" is their constant refrain. Others keep their idealistic dreams and continue to ride roughshod over disappointments, failing to learn the telling lessons of life.

Yet we can also learn to live with constraints. An old African proverb may get us started: "the one who swallows 'udala' (apple) seed must consider the size of one's anus."[28]

While one could get multiple meanings from this rather graphic proverb, the basic meaning is that when we take on an issue or project, we need to think through the consequences of what it might take to see it to completion. Or to put it much more simply: don't take on more than you can fulfil.

This proverb warns us that we should not be too grandiose with our hopes and dreams and that we should understand the relationship between actions and consequences. But it also invites us to live with constraints. It's better not to swallow something if it gets stuck in your system. We might think of Atlas who carried the world on his shoulders, Jesus who suffered for humanity on a cross, or Gandhi who changed the destiny of India through suffering, fasting, and nonviolent resistance. But if we can't hold the weight of the world, bear the suffering of the cross, or endure long periods of fasting, we'd best not swallow such immense seeds!

It is not cowardly to live within the internal constraints that we place on ourselves or to accept legitimate external constraints. Rather, we live with a sober realism, which does not say, "nothing is possible," but rather, "not everything is possible." Since not everything is possible, we have to discern what to strive for and what to let go.

There is nothing defeatist about this stance, as it does not suggest that we surrender to inevitable forces or resign ourselves to our fate. Rather, something very positive and liberating is at play here, which is the realisation that I am not the Messiah. Instead, I am someone with passions, gifts, and concerns, who also has limitations, follies, and stupidities. I can do certain things and make a contribution, but I can't be and do everything.

The simple lesson is: don't try to swallow something that will choke you!

RESPONSIBLE STEWARDSHIP

a spirituality of concern

One can cut large thongs from another person's leather.

We are particular rather than universal creatures, and so our connection to place is important. However, this connection is often seen as prosaic, because we are constantly invited to be on the move, see the world, and become a global citizen.

Because we live in such a highly urban and global world, we are often alienated from nature, disconnected from food production, and fragmented in our local communities.

We live as though we can take everything for granted, as if everything is for the taking—including the earth's fragile resources. Thus we lack a sense of responsible stewardship.

An old thirteenth-century proverb can help us think differently. The French version, "du cuir d'autrui large courroie," and the German, "aus fremden Leder ist gut Riemen schneiden," roughly equates to, "one can cut large thongs from another person's leather."[29]

The basic meaning of this proverb is that it is easy to be generous with what is not ours. Or to push this a little further, it is easy to be irresponsible with what is not ours.

This is rather evident in contemporary culture. One can easily fritter away the boss's time. For public servants with employment security in a highly insecure world, it is easy to be self-focussed and career oriented rather than a true servant of the people. For politicians, it is easy to be more concerned with holding onto power than working hard to achieve the national good. For multinational corporations, it is easy to avoid being good corporate citizens.

But we are all implicated. We take so much granted, and we fail to care well for the natural world.

All of this constitutes a failure in good stewardship. We have grown up with the idea that the world and its resources are simply there for our use and misuse. We take much more than we should and give so little back.

With the increasing loss of a critical sociology, we have abandoned a self-critical approach to life and lost a language that shows our true colours in the mirror. As a result, the word "exploitative" has fallen into disuse, but that word describes all of us.

We take with hardly a care. We use and give little back. We assume that everything is ours when really the world and all it contains is a fragile gift.

God's creation is not our possession, but a gift that sustains us!

Let us stop taking more than is necessary. Let us live simply so that others may simply live.

MAKING WAY

learning to pass the baton

If the rat cannot flee, let it make way for the tortoise.

One can see the world in terms of scarcity or abundance, and this varying outlook has all sorts of consequences. The perspective of scarcity spurs me to fight to get what I need. The outlook of abundance invites me to think about fair distribution. Either way, I am faced with challenges.

One present-day growing anxiety and concern is uncertainty regarding the job market. Employment security is a thing of the past, and our ever-changing workplaces threaten continuity of employment.

Insecurity tends to spawn fear, and fear prompts us to batten down the hatches. In other words, we will do everything we can to hang on to what we have.

However understandable this may be, it is not a good way to live. In our personal lives, this posture locks us in—often with attitudes of resentment. In the workplace, it stifles our productivity.

The African proverb, "if the rat cannot flee, let it make way for the tortoise,"[30] may be a helpful starting point. The basic meaning is that if you get stuck, let others try, or make way for others.

At face value, this is a ridiculous suggestion. In a world of job and myriad other forms of insecurity, the last thing I want to do is to make way for others. In fact, my whole orientation is to hang on desperately to whatever I have.

But to let go or to get out of the way and to face my fears and insecurities head-on may be the most liberating move I have ever made, even though it will be fraught by uncertainties.

To put this in a broader perspective, we will inevitably find ourselves trying to do tasks for which we are not suited, and thus we will need to hand them on to others. As we develop new skills through re-training, we will have to let go of the familiar and move on. As we gain more self-insight and awareness and thus discover more of our inner motivations and giftedness, we will need to follow this new trail. And as we mature, we can more readily hand things on to others and be more inclusive rather than holding things close to our own chest.

To a significant degree, we are exploring the problem of being stuck in a job, role, or task because of fear and insecurity and our failure to take risks, to let go, to move on. We are also exploring the challenge of handing things over to others and getting out of the way.

There is nothing easy in any of this, but we will live a fuller life by taking risks.

CORRUPTION

the strategies of co-option

A fish begins to stink at the head.

Our lives are shaped by personal, familial, institutional, and national spheres. In our personal and familial spheres, we have significant room to make our own choices, although we are influenced by the dominant values of our culture. In the institutional and national dimensions of life, our personal choices are often diminished. In very significant ways, we just have to fit in.

Before too long, we begin to struggle with what is being asked of us in these settings. We become aware that our company, business, or corporation is not always as ethical as we would like it to be. And so we begin to struggle with all sorts of questions. Should I say something? Should I leave? Can I stay and live with my conscience? Should I be a whistleblower and live with the unhappy consequences of taking such a stand? The questions can be endless.

There are two basic starting points in considering this dilemma. First, we are living in less than perfect circumstances and will always be implicated in what is less than good. Thus we have to make some compromises. Second, we are not robots. We have human agency and can do something.

The classic Russian proverb, "a fish begins to stink at the head,"[31] suggests that corruption often occurs at the top and filters down. It is also factual, given the corruption in Russia's national life, a corruption that is also evident elsewhere!

A number of core strategies occur in the corruption process. We do well to heed these, even though we may wish to turn a blind eye and dismiss something as "not my problem."

First, someone above you may seem to favour you without good reason and seek to draw you to himself or herself. This is called "grooming."

Second, you may be asked to do something that is only partly shady. When you agree to do this, you could be setting yourself up for further breaches down the line.

Third, someone above you may ask you to do something that brings you concern or discomfort, and then the person spends time with you to rationalise it or explain it away.

Fourth, you may be asked to do something, and when you express concern, you may be threatened with possible demotion or job loss.

What is most insidious is that within a business or organisation, our values can be slowly eroded when we take on board the idea that it is ultimately not our responsibility, because the responsibility lies with those in power.

However, as this proverb powerfully suggests, the rot affects us as well.

GENEROSITY

a spirituality of grace

*A great man [woman] does not remember
a petty person's trespasses.*

It is a sad reflection on the human condition when we become petty and mean-spirited. This is tragic not only in our personal relationships, but also in the workplace and our institutions. Corporate and communal life functions best when it is based on trust and generosity. To be gracious towards one another is a hallmark of our humanity.

A Chinese proverb expresses this well: "a great man [woman] does not remember a petty person's trespasses."[32] This proverb speaks from the perspective of the well-to-do or powerful in relation to those who are further down the scale of social stratification. A generosity of spirit towards the vulnerable or needy should be commended. But simply to forgive or forget is not the highest form of goodness—for it is even more important to uplift and empower those who are vulnerable.

This proverb raises some further questions. While the strong should be kind to the weak, what is the dynamic at a peer level? And how are the needy to treat one another?

Regarding the first question, life at the peer level can be quite different. Those who are powerful and strong often feel they need to be competitive with those in similar circumstances. They must not show weakness. Thus generosity of heart and a spirit of forgiveness may be more difficult.

And while we may romanticise the poor because of their sense of community and solidarity with one another, they also experience competition because of a scarcity of resources. Having a generous heart here may also be a challenge.

Rather than interpreting this proverb in terms of social differentiation, we might consider two people who are equal, or approximate, in social standing or wealth, and yet a huge chasm divides them in terms of character, ethics, and attitude.

The one, despite his or her greatness, is marked by humility and values kindness. This is expressed in being able to overlook another person's failings and extend forgiveness.

The other has a very different disposition. Power and position has had a corrosive influence, narrowing the arteries of the heart. Arrogance and self-righteousness have become the dominant strains of this person's life, along with an inability to admit mistakes and make things right.

The first has a generous heart, while the second is marked by pettiness. The former is truly great, while the latter is diminished, in spite of his or her outward greatness.

Despite our contemporary quest for much-having and security, our possessions and status can never fully define us, for human well-being is determined by more than material resources or the quest for significance.

Our well-being is sculpted by the practices of generosity and compassion, which ensure human flourishing—not only for the recipient, but also for the giver.

NECESSARY EVIL

ambiguity and discernment

No evil without its advantages.

Most of us do not live with a desire to do harm. Instead, we want to do good and value well-being and peace. Obviously, we all fail in this from time to time.

However, it is one thing to see wrongdoing as undesirable and unfortunate, but it is quite another to see it as something necessary. The phrase, "to wage war in order to make peace," is a case in point of how we use this language.

The ancient Roman phrase, "malum necessarium," and the Dutch, "een noodzakelijk kwaad,"[33] can be translated as "a necessary evil." The English proverb, "no evil without its advantages,"[34] points us in a similar direction.

While we know that good can come out of all sorts of difficult circumstances, it is quite different to consider that evildoing can have a good end. What makes this even more difficult is when we believe that there is a direct relationship between the ends and means. The logic here would suggest that peacemaking strategies produce real peace.

Yet no matter how much we may wrestle with the notion of a necessary evil, it is a fact of life.

We accept that in times of war, a woman will sleep with the enemy to gain information. People working in the secret services use deceit to gain an advantage. Dietrich Bonhoeffer was willing to lie in order to continue his opposition to Hitler. Governments keep their societies as safe as possible through the use of force.

At a more benign level, a doctor may withhold the complete truth about a patient's condition so that the patient and his or her family won't lose hope.

So much of life is marked by ambiguity. Seldom is the path of goodness and righteousness a straight path. We may have to choose Aristotle's wisdom: "of two evils choose the least."[35]

In all its complexity, life does not give us the space to live out what is good in a singular way. Sometimes we have to use a crooked stick to make a straight blow.

One may well say that the death of Christ on the cross was a necessary evil as it brought about the redemption of all humanity.

DILUTION

resisting diminishment

To add water to wine.

Having been involved for over twenty-five years in graduate education, I am increasingly concerned about the quality of the research papers that land on my desk. I am left wondering about my students' study habits and sense that the work has been thrown together too quickly. Speed, rather than depth of reading and reflection, seems to be the underlying motivation.

Of much greater concern, I see signs of this speed-driven motivation everywhere—both in the political domain and the life of the faith community. Short-term gain seems to be the order of the day in politics, and superficiality has gripped the Christian community. Our imaginations have been captured by breadth rather than depth, and convenience rather than principle.

Multiple factors orchestrate this present reality, including the speed of technological communication and innovation. Yet more fundamentally, the art of reflection is being replaced with strategies for effectiveness that lack historical depth, because we have adopted a sceptical stance towards the past and have glorified our present inventiveness. Consequently, trendy superficiality is being promoted as present-day wisdom.

In the Gospel story, Jesus turns water into wine, but in Kierkegaard's critique, the church turns wine into water. The Dutch proverb, "water bij de wijn doen"[36] —"to add water to wine"—is relevant in this discussion. Simply put, it means to water something down, which is a good description for much that is happening in our society.

We see signs of this slippage and the abdication of our long and rich cultural heritage in many spheres: political parties that have pragmatics but no significant ideology, universities that place little emphasis on the humanities, schools that don't teach philosophy, churches that no longer teach doctrine and no longer "form" people in the faith. We have poured a lot of water into the wine glass.

It is time to drink a glass of good, strong red wine. It's time to go back to read and appropriate our rich Greek and Christian roots, the Renaissance and the Reformation, humanism and theological perspectives of the modern era.

Rather than waiting for something to change our institutions, we need to begin the change ourselves, along with others, by reading primary sources, discussing our heritage, learning from philosophy, reading theology, grappling with ethical issues, becoming more critical, living alternatively. Why allow ourselves to be defined by the consumerism of our time when we can live out of much richer traditions?

Our ever-mindless connectivity and communicative superficiality can find richer pastures. Let's look, explore, and drink deeply.

27

PERSISTENCE

a spirituality of perseverance

It is not with the first stroke that the tree falls.

We are all aware that we are living in a fast-paced society, where almost everything is fluid, and change is the order of the day. In this setting, we expect things to happen quickly. Thus with the projects we undertake, we expect quick results.

But to live with such expectations is rather unrealistic. Not everything can happen quickly. Many things require the blessing of time and call for the gift of perseverance.

The Gaelic proverb, "it is not with the first stroke that the tree falls,"[37] is an appropriate reminder. When using an axe, felling a tree calls for much effort.

There are many dimensions of life that call for effort and persistence— building lasting relationships, changing the culture of an organisation, engaging in community development, starting a new business, healing broken friendships, mentoring others, and so on.

Because so much effort is required with such projects, it is important to understand the gestalt of perseverance. In other words, persistence contains a certain logic and has a certain inner shape.

One dimension of the gestalt of perseverance is that the project must be deemed as worthwhile. We are not likely to persevere with something if we think it is a waste of time and effort.

For a project to be worthwhile, we must place a high value on it and believe that we should put effort into it. We will engage in and invest in an activity when we are deeply motivated. This motivation can spring from self-interest, care for others, survival, enhancement, duty, guilt, a sense of spiritual calling, and many other stirrings within our inner being.

Some other dimensions of the gestalt of perseverance include a willingness to persist in the face of opposition and difficulty, along with a powerful hope that things will eventually fall into place.

But not everything we valiantly commit ourselves to will come to a fruitful conclusion. We may persevere, but fail in the end. We may give something our best shot and hang in for a long time, but then realise that success escapes us. Thus to persevere, we must learn the difficult arts of grief and relinquishment.

CONTAGION

a sociology of association

He [she] that touches pitch shall be defiled.

A certain inversion occurs in contemporary culture: the more we emphasise our sense of independence, the more we tend to conform to contemporary values.

This should not surprise us, because we are social creatures. We may want to be unique and different, but we also want to belong to family, friends, nation, and other forms of association.

As a consequence, we live an interesting dialectic—or creative tension—between individuality and group identity. This raises the following question: which tends to be the dominant reality? While some people may be radically individualistic and out of step with the culture of their time, most of us are far more conformist than we realise.

This poses further questions. The Dutch proverb, "wie met pek omgat, word ermee besmet,"[38] may be a challenging point of departure. The English equivalent is "he [she] that touches pitch shall be defiled."

There are at least two ways to make sense of this proverb. First, if we handle unwholesome things, then these things will affect our well-being and values. In other words, external things can pervade our inner being. In the movie *Witness*, which deals with the violence that comes to an Amish community, an Amish grandfather tells his young grandson that a gun in the hand becomes violence in the heart.

Second, if we associate with certain "others" or particular groups, we will be influenced and contaminated by them. We might think immediately of gangs, bikies, and terrorist groups. But we tend not to think about the way that our involvement in the world of business shapes us or the ways we conform to dominant values of a culture.

There are no easy solutions to how we are influenced by the things around us. The challenge is not so much for individuals to try to escape from the dominant culture, but rather to become part of a counter-community that holds more wholesome values.

While this may sound idealistic, let me sound a note of realism. If we do need to handle "pitch," we should make sure to clean our hands. The point here is that we are all implicated in the evil committed by our institutions and societies in some way. Thus we need to find ways of restitution.

More particularly, rather than only handling "pitch," we should also hold in our hands a pitcher of water, bread, healing oil, and the dove of peace.

29

SENSITIVITY

healing words

To sugar the pill.

There seems to be a growing harshness in the way we now communicate. We see verbal slanging matches in parliament, dramatic reporting in the media, terse email communications, blunt directives in the business world, and brutal verbal attacks in social media.

One wonders whether civility has disappeared from our social life.

A proverb may help us to recover a way of speaking that has a healing dimension. The proverb, "dorer la pilule" in French and "de pil vergulden" in Dutch, is literally translated, "to gild the pill," in English, but can be expressed more familiarly as "to sugar the pill."[39]

We can mine various emphases from these words of wisdom. First, we can say something difficult that needs to be said—usually in terms of a corrective—in a straightforward way, but with gentleness. Thus, this communication is not about vagueness but kindness.

Second, if one has done something hurtful to another, then it is appropriate to speak with that person as gently as possible. This is the language of reparation.

A third possible meaning is to use over-the-top language in proposing something preposterous or outlandish. Gilding the lily, indeed!

These meanings all bring us to the common theme of healing words. While cynical and sarcastic language often seems to be the order of the day, we desperately need language that encourages and heals.

Though we might dismissively say that words don't matter as much as deeds, words do carry our heart and have consequences!

Healing words do not avoid, downplay, or mask life's difficulties or harsh realities. Neither do they scurry over the top of something nor descend into hollow pieties.

Rather, healing words acknowledge pain and disappointment, but speak hope into the dungeon of chaos. Healing words can reach over the abyss of the distance we create with our deafening refrains, "no one knows what I am going through," or "no one has suffered like me."

Thus healing words that emerge from a gentle and concerned heart build a bridge over troubled waters.

30

DESIRE

a spirituality of longing

Where there is desire, there is ability.

To live wanting everything is clearly a problem. And no matter how hard one tries, disappointment will come—as may a breakdown or burnout.

To live wanting nothing is also a problem. This is skating at the edges of death. But even at the edges of death, there is normally the desire to be free from pain, or to have one last time with loved ones, or to go to heaven, along with many other needs and desires.

The Spanish proverb, "donda hay gana, hay maña,"[40] which means, "where there is desire, there is ability," may be a good starting point to think more about this topic.

As humans, we are fundamentally creatures of desire. Put in other words, we long for something. Often, we long for many things—and happiness is but one of our desires.

So why can't we accept what is, rather than long for what could be? Do our longings mean that we see ourselves as incomplete or deprived in some way? Do our desires seek to meet our basic needs? Or do our longings help us progress, because we sense that things could be better? Or might our desires move us towards transcendence, which helps us to understand the spiritual or religious impulses in the human heart?

These are all questions worth pondering, and we should try to make some sense of our desires so they do not become compulsions that drive us relentlessly. Thus we might ask, towards what end should our desires be directed—our basic needs? well-being? much-having? Or should our desires be directed toward some higher goals—altruism? the common good? the quest for justice?

While the questions are endless, the thrust of this Spanish proverb gets to the point: desire gives ability. Being creatures of desire gives us momentum and energy.

The proverb does not suggest how to orient our desires, but we each need to find our answers to this challenging question. The very fact that we are creatures of desire calls us to discern and make choices. As such, an ethical imperative lies within us and upon us, which can be seen either as a burden or an invitation.

If we see this imperative as an invitation, the power of choice and human agency lies within our grasp. Desire can undo the power of fate and the biology of our human condition by moving us to be something better than we imagined.

WOUNDED

a spirituality of suffering

One man [woman] who's been flogged
is worth two who haven't.

I think we all understand that a person who has only experienced privilege and fair-weather sailing is quite different from someone who has struggled in life and been "wounded" in the process. Life's difficulties and sorrows have a way of breaking and remaking us.

The Russian proverb, "one man [woman] who's been flogged is worth two who haven't,"[41] is rather to the point. While this can be understood in a number of ways, two meanings stand out. First, the person who's been flogged might have been a wrongdoer who, after being punished, has learned his or her lesson. Second, the person might have criticised those in power and been unjustly punished.

A more general but related point is that we can learn much from being "bloodied" by life. And so it follows that if there is anyone that we should look to for wisdom, it is a person with a limp.

This reflection is inspired by the biblical story of Jacob, a patriarch of the Jewish faith, who wrestles with an "angel" and ends up with a limp.

This encounter marks an important transition point in Jacob's life, when Jacob—the self-determined and self-sufficient wheeler, dealer, and schemer—receives a strange "flogging" that forges humility within him and changes him forever.

We are not merely self-made by our expertise and natural ability, for we are also shaped by others and by both the good things that come our way as well as the difficulties we experience.

While difficulty and suffering may bear the unproductive fruits of cynicism and withdrawal, such "floggings" can also bear good fruit. The greatest fruit is wisdom that is marked by humility and deep care for others who struggle with life's difficulties and unfairness.

A wise person both understands and empathises. A wise person won't dump cheap answers and solutions on others, nor wave a quick-fix wand, but will journey alongside others through pain and difficulties.

A "wounded" person will walk the long mile with others—only ever so slowly!

IN RESERVE

the gentle art of withholding

Do not all you can; spend not all you have;
believe not all you hear; and tell not all you know.

Some people advocate that one should engage issues and causes "boots and all." I am concerned about this approach to life, which may say a lot about the kind of person I am.

I am much more on the wavelength of the nineteenth-century English saying, "do not all you can; spend not all you have; believe not all you hear; and tell not all you know."[42]

There are a number of reasons why I like this practical wisdom. First, gushing everything out, so to speak, is over the top and may well confuse or overwhelm others. Second, giving our all in a situation may well be an immature reaction on our part, reflecting our need to be needed. Third, we need to hold something in reserve. What about the next day and the day after that? Most helping and giving strategies are long-term rather than geared for immediate solutions.

Even more importantly, we must not lose ourselves in the process of caring for and helping others. We need to guard the sacredness of our being, and therefore we cannot say or do everything. Self-care is an important consideration in the art of self-giving.

This wise saying also reflects the significant need for timing and discernment. We need to speak and act in appropriate ways at the right time. Gentle rain may be more appropriate than a gushing stream.

The seventeenth-century English proverb is to the point here: "to give and keep, there is a need for wit [wisdom/discernment]."[43] In the art of giving or withholding, discernment is necessary.

There are many good reasons for this. What *we* desire to give may not be appropriate. We need to give what the other is willing to receive.

Sometimes, we may not need to say or do something, but rather to listen attentively. During these times, we withhold speech or action—not because we are being stingy, but because it is best for the other.

To be discerning means to hold something back so that we can internally reflect and reason within ourselves. In this reflective space, we attend to the heartbeat of what is best for the other.

Thus the art of discerning what to do or not to do calls us to move slowly rather than to dive in where angels fear to tread.

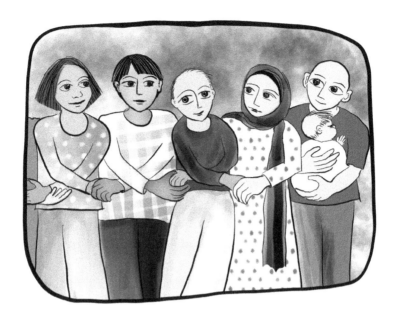

<u>33</u>

UNITY

the power of cooperation

A horde of ants can conquer a poisonous snake.

Many of us have experienced an employment or organisational environment marked by joy and cooperation. Not only did we go to work with anticipation and energy, but so much got done—often with seeming little effort.

Most of us have also experienced the opposite: lack of good leadership, unclear goals, bickering, jealousies, and a lack of cooperation. What a pain to go daily to such a setting!

Some of us have also been part of social protest movements, when a common focus propelled us forward—only to see that shattered further down the line due to fragmentation and seemingly irresolvable conflict.

In so much of the experience of life, the magic of holding a common purpose and direction soon evaporates. How tragic this is!

The Chinese proverb, "a horde of ants can conquer a poisonous snake,"[44] can help us think more about this matter. The proverb gives a clear image of seemingly little power harming a much larger foe by working cooperatively. Said another way, there is strength in unity.

In the so-called Arab Spring, ordinary citizens were able to mobilise protest movements through social media, which brought down various dictators. The fact that they were not able to consolidate their gains does not take away from the wisdom of this proverb.

While there are various dimensions that we could explore in relation to this proverb, I will focus on the significance that unity can play in reaching a certain goal.

There are some important dimensions to the matter of achieving unity and understanding its nature and outcomes.

While unity can be—and often is—imposed from above with some sort of threat, such unity is finally self-defeating. Cracks appear, resentment builds, and those in power increase their demands and threats only to overreach, which leads to some sort of collapse.

Unity is best achieved by casting a vision that resonates with the values and hopes of all the players. Unity is deepened when all feel that they are making a contribution and see the benefits for themselves and others.

Thus unity is a process that has to be won amidst the chaos and fragmentation that so readily bubble to the surface.

While unity may be more easily achieved at the beginning of a movement, it is harder to maintain further down the road. Thus unity needs both creativity and maintenance.

Maintaining unity involves ongoing affirmation and the fine-tuning of goals, along with concomitant flexibility. Unity also requires an ongoing ability to see the value of the movement while also holding the memory of the key markers that sparked the journey together. Moreover, it involves dealing with failures and losses, facing new challenges, and the willingness to suffer for one's vision and cause.

It's remarkable what people with a common purpose can achieve!

PEACE

inner and outward dimensions

Peace is not the absence of war, it is a virtue, a state of mind, a disposition of benevolence, confidence and justice.

We are not living in a peaceful world. Wars continue, and everywhere there are racial conflicts and ethnic tensions. The spectres of fear have invaded the very fabric of our fragile inner life. Ours is an age of anxiety, and these anxieties have spread their tentacles into every aspect of our lives. Our very identity seems to be threatened.

Perhaps it should not surprise us that we are always on guard and unsettled. Tensions rule us rather than the goodness of the peaceable kingdom. These tensions may express themselves not only in terms of irritability, but also in various forms of aggression. The tragedy of family violence is but one indicator of these inner fissures.

Our longing for relief is a chronic inner ache, and the fact that peace seems so distant adds to our sense of hopelessness.

One critical issue is, where do we look for peace? Even more importantly, to *whom* do we look for peace?

We often tend to look elsewhere, thinking that external conditions of peace will translate to an inner reality of peace. But this may make peace an impossible dream.

The Dutch philosopher Baruch Spinoza (1632–1677) points us in another direction, reminding us that "peace is not the absence of war, it is a virtue, a state of mind, a disposition of benevolence, confidence and justice."[45] In other words, Spinoza suggests that peace is first and foremost an inner sculpture, an inner state of well-being. He also makes the point that such peace is possible even in the face of external conditions to the contrary.

Coming to an inner sense of peace is a carefully woven tapestry with delicate designs and myriad colours. It will include living with a profound sense of self-acceptance, the joy of gratitude, honouring the dignity and worth of others, rejecting having power *over* others, and seeing much of life as a gift rather than the product of self-achievement.

Thus while we have to play our part in weaving this tapestry, peace is also a gift of the spirit.

For Spinoza, however, this inner peace not only has an inward focus, but also has an outward orientation, generating benevolence and justice.

Thus the nature of inner peace is characterised by an outward movement. Whatever peace I have, I wish to share, because this inner construction and gift of peace is sustained by sharing it with others. Peace is not simply personal, for its very nature is communal.

GIVING

a spirituality of sharing

The one who gives to another bestows on oneself.

Our present-day culture is not oriented towards a strong sense of communalism and generosity. We can't have the former without the latter, for community cannot exist without self-giving and sharing.

Rather, our age is oriented towards a self-focused individualism. Our culture constantly promotes the idea that we should only be concerned about ourselves because no one else will look after us. Thus the mantra of our times is that self-effort promotes well-being.

Yet this is a faulty perspective, since so much of life is interrelated and intertwined. Our family life, work-a-day world, and the very fabric of society all point towards forms of cooperation and interrelatedness.

One important theme in this is that self-concern does not promote human flourishing, for self-giving is as important as receiving. In acts of care and generosity, we both bless others and enrich ourselves. The seventeenth-century English proverb, "the one who gives to another bestows on oneself,"[46] reflects this insight.

We are concerned here with the kind of person we are *becoming* through certain acts of goodness. We cannot live into greater well-being if we shrink our personal world to the narrow confines of self-focus. For narrowing the arteries of our hearts leads to all sorts of inner constrictions.

We need to engage in becoming a fuller and expanded self. This does not take place merely through further education and professional enhancement, though these are important.

Rather, to become the person we are called and invited to become, we must embrace a counter-intuitive reality. The dominant logic of our time is that we live in a world of limitation and threats, and so we need to gain for ourselves as much as we can in order to ensure our well-being. Yet according to a counter-intuitive logic, we live in a world of abundance, where our well-being is about both giving and taking, sharing and receiving.

This proverb clearly reflects the latter vision of life. Taking is, in the end, self-defeating. Though we may accumulate much, we shrivel the membranes of our inner being in the process. A life of both receiving and giving shapes us into people "of the heart," rather than people of mean calculation.

Blessing others makes us richer in the quest for generosity of heart, and this is intrinsic to becoming the kind of people that better the human community—not simply for survival, but for human flourishing.

36

UNREALITY

when hope is folly

To drag solutions out of nowhere.

One of the most difficult questions in life has to do with the relationship between faith and folly or hope and unreality. Some people believe that faith and hope are always ill-founded and should be discarded. But others believe that such a presumption overplays rationality and underplays intuition and the human propensity towards hope in the face of despair. The old English proverb, "if it were not for hope, the heart would break,"[47] highlights this sentiment.

So should we continue to hope even though our hopes may be dashed? Or is hope some sort of opium, akin to Karl Marx's dictum that religion is an opium that sidetracks us from concern for *this* world? Of course, the counter-question is, can we live well in this world without religion or without hope?

In attempting to move forward, we need to acknowledge that we are skating on thin ice and have to negotiate some difficult matters.

The Dutch proverb, "legers uit de grond stampen,"[48] literally means to "stamp armies out of the ground." Colloquially, we might say this means "to drag solutions out of nowhere," or "to suck answers out of your thumb." Most simply put, it is to believe in unrealistic or magical solutions, which is akin to calling "heavenly" armies out of nowhere to conquer the foe.

This is precisely the difficulty, for how can we distinguish between hope and sheer folly? between abandoning a hopeless cause or continuing against all odds?

Though there are no neat answers, and there is no magic formula, hope and folly are nearer to one another than we may readily acknowledge, for sometimes hope may seem to be sheer folly. While some press on with their hopes, causes and concerns regardless of the odds, others have long given up.

So is this then a matter of personal choice, related to the kind of people we are? Might someone with an easy-going personality abandon ship sooner than a more high-principled person? Or is it more about the nature of the causes we espouse? Does the movement we are a part of play a part in our decision to press on against all odds? In terms of our values, are some negotiable, while others are not? What role does our inner world of intuition, faith, and hope play?

The questions are endless, but if a cause is significant—such as seeking to prevent the arbitrary killing of our fellow human beings—then we should press on, whether we are successful or not. In such circumstances, drumming up magical helpers might be debilitating.

Thus it may be best to leave these hoped-for "armies" in the ground, for to summon them is sheer folly.

37

RECEPTIVITY

a spirituality of openness

Nothing can get into a closed fist

The flow of life requires receptivity and openness, for life is not only about giving, but also receiving. The ability to receive calls for humility and vulnerability.

The more capable we are and the greater our resources, the more we can think that we don't need anything from others. But we all need to be in relationship with others. We all need love, advice, and encouragement. We need others in order to run a business. We all need the farmer, the motor mechanic, and the medical doctor.

Since life is a web of sacred connectedness, we need to be receptive to its responsibilities, challenges, and mystery. Embracing life's mystery requires curiosity and openness. The Gaelic proverb, "nothing can get into a closed fist,"[49] can help us think more about the gentle art of receptivity.

Many people live with their fists closed and shut themselves down in relating to others. Those who have been wounded create barriers to shut others out. Some assume that what others seek to give is only a self-serving attempt to fulfil unmet needs.

There is also the dynamic of obligation—which is stronger in some cultures than others—when we sense that any help, care, or gifts we receive needs to be reciprocated in some way.

Thus there are both good and bad reasons for wanting to live with a closed fist. There is the plain sense, "I don't need or want what you wish to give."

And yet, there is a curious mystery when we live with an open hand. We are not only willing to admit that we may need things from others—which will vary with the flow of life—but also that we are open to what may come our way unexpectedly. If we wish to remain open to surprise, then our hearts and hands need to be open—even extended.

An open hand requires both awareness and discernment. We need to be aware of our needs and discerning about to whom and to what we are willing to open our hands.

A closed fist may tragically diminish our lives as we stagnate around habits and entrenched opinions. To live well, we need to be continually revitalised and renewed, which calls for receptivity.

38

OPPOSITION

the reality of conflict

If the Tao or Buddha rises one foot, the demon rises ten.

If our world were stationary and stagnant, change and opposition would be a non-issue. But our world is ever-changing, and so resistance and opposition can be expected.

While we may wish for everything to be plain sailing, working for change seems to attract opposition. This should not surprise us, since people tend to prefer the status quo to uncertain change. The question is, how can we be sure that the projected change will be for the better?

The Chinese proverb, "if the Tao or Buddha rises one foot, the demon rises ten,"[50] is an appropriate starting point for further reflection. This proverb can mean that those who seek to do good in the world are outnumbered by those who wish to do evil. Or it can mean that any move towards the good will be countered by those seeking the opposite. It can also mean that the attempt to solve one problem will lead to the emergence of other problems.

In interpreting this proverb, I wish to make several points. First, we should not accept a metaphysical dualism. The universe is not the arena of two powerful but balanced spiritual forces. Nor is evil the most powerful force in the universe. Most religions hold that goodness and love are the most powerful forces, but evil is always a possibility.

Second, the more that there are movements for good at work in the world, the more the nature of evil will be exposed. The greater the light, the more darkness will be revealed.

Third, the nature of what is good in our world can be understood as initiated by humans and inspired and sustained by the spirit. Thus, goodness has a spiritual dimension, as does evil. Evil is what we do, but we can be seduced by dark spiritual forces.

Fourth, there are times in history when evil seems so powerful. We think of the evils of war, poverty, and injustice, when the forces of darkness are in top gear. This Chinese proverb highlights how the "demon" rises ten feet during these times.

But we can also turn this proverb on its head: when the demon rises ten feet, goodness only needs to rise one foot. We can make this move because the more powerful evil becomes, the more unsustainable it becomes, for it carries within itself the seeds of its own destruction. Only goodness is self-sustaining.

More critically, when the demon rises ten feet, it shows its true colours. What is most dangerous for us is when the demon slumbers, and we fail to discern its presence.

39

ENVY

a bitter poison

The cow of another always has a bigger udder.

Some people have little motivation and don't long for much at all, but seem to be content with whatever they have.

Yet our society does not want us to live this way. The mantra is that what we have is not enough. When we strive to get more and gain it, we are told that it can't possibly satisfy us, because we need something else. Though this is clearly good for the economy, whether it is good for us personally is another matter.

Mixed in with the mantra of much-having is the politics of envy. If I can become more envious, I will strive harder to get what other people have and what think I need or deserve.

The Swedish proverb, "the cow of another always has a bigger udder," reflects this dynamic.[51] An English approximate is, "the envious person waxes lean with the fatness of his/her neighbour."[52]

Yet envy can be a hard taskmaster, and other things can move us towards productivity and effectiveness, such as self-survival and altruism.

One problem with the politics of envy is that it can so easily become a much more dangerous cocktail. Envy can drive us to try to get what someone else has at any cost and in any way. The tentacles of this reach far and wide.

But there is also an inverse problem associated with envy, as it can lead to self-loathing. If I never attain what I envy in others, I begin to weave the narrative that I am less than others, which can lead to myriad self-deprecating scenarios. *I am unfortunate. The gods aren't smiling upon me. I am badly done by. Life is not fair.* And so on.

Envy is a bitter poison that needs to be lanced out of our system and replaced by better motivations.

One positive way to move forward is to express our giftedness, steward our resources, and enhance a future—both for ourselves and for others.

40

IMAGINATION

a spirituality of seeing

In a good book the best is between the lines.

We live in a world with many freedoms, but also with powerful cultural and social constraints and all-pervasive influences. As a result, we often feel more "bound" than free, which can easily undermine our creativity and make life seem humdrum, boring, and stale. This is hardly a recipe for human flourishing.

To live well, we need to be able to dream and imagine a better existence than the one we are presently experiencing.

The Swedish proverb, "in a good book the best is between the lines,"[53] may be a good starting point to help us think about the power of the imagination by providing us with the insight that we need to see more than what is in front of us.

Whether one reads a book or a life, much is left to the imagination. A good book does not exhaustively explain everything, but rather evokes a "world" that we may want to inhabit or change.

To read a book or a life "between the lines" suggests both an expansive reading—there is more to the story—and a critical reading—not everything should necessarily be believed or taken on board.

Yet the most productive way to read "between the lines" is when a book or life brings us into the realm of something new or evokes some possibility we have not thought about before.

This reflects the link between inspiration and imagination. Inspiration is a fruit of the spirit. Imagination is initiated by the spirit and moves us beyond our present horizons. When we move beyond our socially-constructed self, we begin to see how things could be different.

This experience brings us to the borderlands of life's normal realities and invites us to take a "leap of faith," which requires courage to leave what is "old and familiar" in order to enter the terrain of the unexplored.

Many hesitate at this point, and some abandon their dreams. Others are fearful. To pursue the dream is a risk, but there are only two alternatives: shut down or start the journey and begin to explore.

True freedom is the gift for those who start the journey and pursue the pathways of their imagination.

41

FLEXIBILITY

overcoming rigidity

The reed before the wind lives on, while mighty oaks do fall.

In our swiftly changing world, we are caught between two good impulses. The first is to find solid ground under our feet, which has to do with maintaining core values and stability. The second is to be as flexible as possible so that we can adjust to the changing realities of life.

The English proverb, "the reed before the wind lives on, while mighty oaks do fall,"[54] is a relevant and challenging proverb that can help us think more about this topic.

Rigidity can be a structural or organisational reality as well as a state of mind and even, in some cases, a personality trait.

Yet flexibility does not suggest that we are blown about by the wind without fixed values, that we are overly compliant, or that we are committed to a radical relativism. Rather, being flexible means that we are versatile and adaptable. When we are supple, we can move and adjust without breaking.

We should enhance and develop this wonderful quality, which is relevant for every dimension of life.

We can be flexible in a conversation by following the back-and-forth movement as it unfolds rather than simply making up our mind beforehand about what we are going to say. Though we may say similar things, we can communicate them in an entirely different way.

We can be flexible in projects as well. No matter how well we envision something and plan its implementation, we will need to make adjustments to the plan as we go along, since we can't possibly take account of all the contingencies that may occur.

The art of adaptability is also called for in life's crises—whether they be more personal, as with health issues, or more communal, as when a natural disaster or armed conflict impacts our lives. In light of these events, we will need to make major adjustments—both practical ones relating to our changing circumstances as well as existential ones in order to make new meaning of our lives.

Finally, flexibility is needed in the aging process, particularly when our "three score years and ten" weigh heavily upon us, and rigorous rigidity may set in. We can no longer do what we were previously capable of doing, which calls for a gentle flexibility in making adjustments without giving up or administering harsh self-recriminations.

Flexibility is an acknowledgement of life's dynamic and ever-changing reality. It's an art we need to learn if we wish to live well.

42

FATE

living well with mystery

One's illness can be cured, but one's fate cannot.

In the West, many people have adopted an agnostic view regarding the role of the world religions in their daily lives. Yet many still explore various spiritualities and grapple with how to make transcendental sense of their lives.

As part of this quest to make sense of life beyond the pragmatic and mundane, some wonder if there are larger forces at work than those that are simply shaped by personal choice.

Some fairly obvious forces are our biology and familial formation, along with the larger cultural movements in our lives. For example, we might inherit a certain biological weakness and end up dying of cancer in a similar way to a grandparent, father, or mother. Or we might observe the way that certain mishaps or tragedies repeat themselves within our family system. So often there seems to be a strange repetition in one's offspring— not only of abilities and virtues, but also of folly and stupidity.

So we struggle with notions of inevitability and fate. The Chinese proverb, "one's illness can be cured, but one's fate cannot,"[55] suggests that fate is a powerful determinant.

The difficulty with the notion of fate is that it presupposes that impersonal predeterminate forces are at work in our world for all eternity, and so certain things are destined to happen and are preordained. Thus fate leads inexorably to fatalism.

There are alternatives to such an ironclad view. One alternative is to replace impersonal fate with a personal God. Thus fate becomes providence, and the phenomenon of these strange repetitions becomes some sort of punishment or trial.

Another alternative is to suggest that both psychological tendencies and predispositions to certain illnesses are biologically inherited—along with much more than we currently understand.

But however we seek to make sense of all this, we need to grapple with the fact that life is about more than our personal choices, and so we are not as free as we might think.

Moreover, if we want to avoid the repetition of folly and stupidity in our children's lives, we must face the challenge of living as well as we can in order to pass on goodness and wisdom to the next generation.

One important factor in this is to believe that healing, redemption, and transformation are possible. Otherwise, we are doomed to the endless repetition of our mistakes.

43

TROUBLING OURSELVES

a spirituality of self-reflection

Most of us trouble others, but few like to trouble themselves.

While there may be some exceptions, most of us are buffeted by the shifting winds of life, which can sweep into the workplace and the economy of our country through economic and natural disasters and personal and familial mishaps. When particularly heavy winds blow, there can be much damage.

Thus we often become self-protective. Some become isolationist or cynical. Many of us, in some way or other, begin to see the world around us in ever-threatening ways and begin to live by the mantra that life is unfair.

One outcome of this is that we can become more reactive to others and less self-reflective.

The Filipino proverb, "most of us trouble others, but few like to trouble themselves,"[56] is a helpful start to further exploring this matter. Proverbs, while reflecting cultural specifics, also have transnational relevance.

To trouble oneself is hardly anyone's favourite pastime. Most likely, we so seldom trouble ourselves that we don't have a good starting point for getting this journey underway.

Gaining self-insight is not usually the result of a blinding light, a revelatory dream, or an unexpected experience that opens a window for us—although these may happen. Most often, gaining self-insight is hard work.

We can begin the work of self-reflection by thinking about the ways we have been wounded in the journey of life. From such wounding, we tend to react, compensate, become defensive, and live out many other unhelpful responses.

We may also need to reflect on the weary burdens that such reactions have brought into our lives as well as others' lives, allowing our reactions to others to act as a mirror. In this way, our foolish reactions can come to our aid.

But possibly the best way to trouble ourselves is to open our lives to a trusted friend, mentor, or guide, who can reflect back to us the places where we are most blind.

As we begin this healing journey, we must be gentle rather than harsh with ourselves. We must tread carefully in the membranes of our inner being!

<u>44</u>

SUSTAINABILITY

a spirituality of substance

Don't walk or skate on ice that has frozen only one night.

Proverbs usually carry layers of meaning, and so they are a rich resource of practical wisdom that can open up a range of interpretive possibilities.

The Dutch proverb, "niet over een nacht ijs gaan," which roughly means, "don't walk or skate on ice that has frozen only one night,"[57] has such a range of meanings. It may beckon us to heed the call not to be foolhardy or stubborn by taking risks that can lead to harm. This invites us to check things out before taking any action—as we would check the thickness of ice before trying to skate on it.

Another possible meaning is to make sure that whatever we embark on is sustainable. To slightly change the image, we must make sure that there is solid ground under our feet—substance to whatever we say and do.

This call has particular relevance for where we are at this point in history. In our fast-changing social landscape and with current expectations in the way we communicate, so much is said and done in a hurry. We see this exemplified in one president's foreign policy via Twitter.

Though fast communication and project completion may seem wonderfully attractive, there are several problems. First, we may readily extend the adrenalin "rush" from such a swift pace to other domains of life—a love affair, business venture, quick-fix solutions to major societal issues and problems, and so on.

We may also assume that we can change ourselves quickly or constantly reinvent ourselves. Sociologist, Zygmunt Bauman, calls this the creation of the palimpsest self, where we think that we can rewrite our lives—our fundamental way of being in the world—many times on the same parchment.

Whether we are working on our own sense of identity, a business venture, or social and political change, who we are and what we are seeking to do needs depth and substance. But such substance does not fall quickly into our lap. The fifteenth-century English proverb, "sudden rising has a sudden fall," issues a stern warning in this regard.[58]

To gain depth about who we are and how we operate in the world, we need to sculpt our inner being over the long term by nurturing daily habits of the heart. Our character is forged through reflection, patience, suffering, and learning from our mistakes.

Our challenge is to make sure that there is ground under our feet and that there is integrity in what we think and say, in our way of being and acting in the world. In this way, we cultivate substance in our lives—not mere latte froth.

THE UNEXPECTED

a spirituality of surprise

A cow may catch a hare;
a blind person may chance to hit the mark.

With the notions that the gods have failed us and the spirit "world" is an ancient worldview that is no longer sustainable in the modern world, our age has become more and more functional and pragmatic. We see everything through the prism of our own making and achievements. The world is no longer "charged with the grandeur of God," as the nineteenth-century English poet G.M. Hopkins writes, but is a world that we are shaping and using.

One of the consequences of this anthropocentric worldview is that everything depends on us and our abilities. A certain "magic" has disappeared from our world, and we are no longer open to surprise.

But surprise can catch us unawares. The twelfth-century Dutch proverb, "men kan niet weten hoe een koe een has vangt," which can be roughly translated, "we can't understand how a cow can catch a hare," illustrates this. The French approximation is, "une vache prend bien un lièvre," and in English, "a cow may catch a hare; a blind person may chance to hit the mark."[59] Indeed, though such occurrences are not likely, they can happen.

Whatever is strange and unexpected is a counterpoint to the world of predictability—and remaining open to such surprising possibilities may serve us well.

Our world is much bigger than each of us, and so much happens that is beyond our control and achievements, our willing and doing. In fact, much of what we do has unforeseen and unintended consequences—and is therefore beyond predictability.

Moreover, whether we like it or not, strange and unexpected things happen—and sometimes they happen to us. The English proverb, "fact is stranger than fiction," comes with an explanation that "things happen sometimes that never entered into the mind of man [woman] to imagine or invent."[60]

These dynamics suggest that we need to live with a much greater sense of openness and humility. This does not mean that we should embrace an ethic of irresponsibility, but rather a life of thoughtful responsibility that remains open to surprises.

And when strange or unexpected things come our way, we can be prepared to laugh—especially at ourselves.

<u>46</u>

MIND GAMES

a spirituality of resistance

The most potent weapon in the hand of the oppressor
is the mind of the oppressed.

We are all becoming more aware of the fact that we are living in a surveillance society, where so much of what we do is recorded for national safety and commercial exploitation.

We are also increasingly aware of the multiple ways in which we are being influenced by the commercial, cultural, and political elite in our respective countries. We are living in a world of propaganda and mind games.

Our challenge is to maintain a sense of freedom and self-determination amidst these circumstances. But is this even possible? Are we simply the victims of the larger forces at work in our world? Should we just give up?

Throughout history, a very long tradition of women and men have demonstrated that we should not succumb, but rather can and should resist. Saint Ambrose resisted the power abuses of the Roman imperium. Martin Luther resisted the abuses in the church of his day. Gandhi resisted the oppressive power of colonialism. Martin Luther King Jr. resisted systemic racism, poverty, and the war economy. Dorothy Day resisted the neglect of the poor.

Steve Biko (1946–1977), the South African freedom fighter against the Apartheid regime, pointed out that when we resist those in power, we need to counter "the most potent weapon in the hand of the oppressor. . . the mind of the oppressed."[61]

This wise observation points to the fact that what is most important is not how powerful the opposition is, nor how small or big a particular issue is. More fundamentally, our central concern is whether we can resist the mind games of those in power and hold to our values and perspectives no matter what—even to the point of ultimate sacrifice.

The mind games of the powerful usually rotate around some core self-justifications: we are the proper authority; we know the big picture; we are doing what is best for law and order; we know what is best for the country; the list goes on and on.

The charges levelled against the opposition are also boringly familiar: you are subversives; you have no legitimacy; you are creating chaos; you are self-serving, and so on.

To remain firm in our opposition, we need to hold the basic conviction that celebrates justice for all rather than privilege for the few. To hold this conviction resolutely, we need companions on the journey. To be countercultural, we need a counter-community. The greatest threat for any counter-community is to become divided, co-opted, and scattered to the four winds.

47

ATTACHMENT

a spirituality of stability

Staying means attachment.

Not so very long ago, many people stayed for the whole of their lives in a particular neighbourhood, remained in the same job, did business with the same bank, and had their cars serviced in the same garage. Moreover, people tended to remain loyal to their church and political party.

Such a world has largely disappeared. These days a person may have four or five major career changes and work for multiple employers. Many people frequently relocate in terms of housing and are fickle about loyalties to associations, parties, and institutions.

But rather than simply lauding the fluidity that is so much a part of contemporary life, it may be worthwhile to think about the notion of stability.

The Dutch proverb, "blijven doet beklijven,"[62] which is roughly translated, "staying means attachment," can be a helpful starting point. The basic meaning is that if one stays in a particular role or position for a long time, one gains depth of experience and security. But, of course, the negative side of this is that one might become stuck in a rut.

The opposite of stability is expressed in the fourteenth-century English proverb: "a rolling stone gathers no moss."[63] Here the idea is to be always on the move, which characterises so much of our contemporary society.

Though there is value in thinking more about stability in our fluid age, I am certainly not suggesting that people hang in where a situation is destructive.

Yet whether one thinks in terms of relationship, place, or vocation, two obvious benefits of stability are continuity and security. Rather than assuming that familiarity breeds contempt, we might consider how familiarity and continuity lead to depth and wisdom.

Stability in relationships allows us to grow through both good times and difficulties together. Stability in our work environments allows trust and understanding to develop. Stability in vocation nurtures growth in expertise.

The concept of stability is central to Benedictine spirituality. Saint Benedict (c. 480–c. 550) had the profound spiritual insight that monks in a community might readily desire to go to another monastery when faced with challenges. The idea that the grass is greener on the other side of the fence is generic to our humanity. Thus a Benedictine monk learned the notion of stability during his formation and made vows to reflect that commitment.

At this point in the twenty-first century, we might learn something from the monks!

48

DEFLATED

a life filled with tears and broken dreams

Empty sacks will never stand upright.

In the last decades, millions of those living in abject poverty in India and China have experienced social and economic uplift. However, poverty continues in many parts of Asia—including both China and India—as well as in Africa and many other places around the world. We have a long way to go until *all* can live with their basic needs met.

Moreover, in many developed countries, the gap between the rich and poor is widening, and some in the middle class are becoming the working-class poor. In the future, with the further robotization of the work force, many people will become completely dependent on welfare. It is dehumanising to be poor and out of work.

The seventeenth-century Italian proverb, "Sacco vuoto non può stare piedi," passed into the English language as, "empty sacks will never stand upright."[64] This describes those who have been impacted by life's misfortunes and left with nothing. Benjamin Franklin used this proverb to suggest that the poor become devoid of spirit and virtue and thus deflated in their humanity.[65]

While Franklin's generalisation is incorrect, since there is overwhelming evidence that the world's poor continue to struggle in hope and make the best of difficult circumstances, it is true that poverty is debilitating—particularly for children.

This proverb evokes the image of having your "guts kicked in." The image of "having the wind knocked out of your sails" is far too benign.

Having no real life options deadens us. Yet so many in our world experience the daily grind of survival, working long hours in menial jobs, where they often get ripped off and receive less than the minimum daily wage. Though there may be food on the table, the house is in a slum, with illegal water and electricity. There is no extra money to cover a sudden illness or to mark a celebration, such as a birth or wedding.

Though such a life is hard, and the future is bleak, many live this way with dignity. The shell of such a life is like an empty sack, containing only tears and broken dreams. But these don't inflate the sack!

It is important for us to consider how we regard ourselves with reference to those who live this way. If we're honest, we may admit that we're indifferent—perhaps callous. But in responding this way, we demean ourselves.

For the poor invite us to helpfulness and generosity. Thus they seek to humanise us—lest we, too, become empty sacks.

49

GENDER EQUALITY

nurturing women's wisdom

Women hold up half the sky.

In Western culture, a long patriarchal history has marginalised women. Even Aristotle, an enlightened soul, put women on a lower rung in the social order.

Though there was an egalitarian impulse in early Christianity, the tradition soon placed women in a subordinate position within the family, society, and the church. Even today, many churches prohibit women from holding positions of leadership. Globally, much still needs to change regarding equality for women.

The Chinese proverb, "women hold up half the sky,"[66] points us in another direction. In modern China, this was a favourite saying of Mao Zedong. In both past and present revolutionary movements, including renewal movements in the church, women have played key roles.

Yet women don't merely hold up half the sky, for they hold up a much greater portion. They not only hold significant roles in contemporary society, but they also continue to play a key role in the home and with their children.

The old typifications of women as nurturers and men as tough, or women playing the "soft" role in society and men doing the hard tasks are no longer credible. For women not only play similar roles as men in society, but they also make distinctive contributions.

One distinctive contribution is what we might call "women's wisdom." While I do not want to overplay the biology of birthing or nurturing infants, women seem to display a more grounded and integrated wisdom. Having lived and worked in Asia for many years, my basic observation is that women achieve much in both home and society while men seem to get much of the credit.

The advent of feminist theology, which reflects "women's wisdom," has been a great blessing to present-day Christianity, helping us to remain sensitive to the role of women in the biblical story, while letting go of the image of God as an old patriarch in the sky. The church is not a patriarchal and hierarchical institution, but a pilgrim people gathering as a church "in the round."

Yet there is still a long way to go, for there are glass ceilings and blockages wherever patriarchal attitudes linger, particularly in the fragile egos of some men.

In Genesis, the first book of the Bible, both women and men were made in the image of God and given the cultural mandate to be fruitful, multiply, fill the earth, and care for it.

Society is not only man's business, and the home is not only women's business. Both men and women have a part to play in the home, the church, other institutions, and society.

Women seem to hold up more than half the sky because women often give so much support to men and yet get so little in return.

<u>50</u>

FORGETTING

commitments made in crisis

The danger past, God is forgotten.[67]

Though there are several fundamental truths about our human condition, the most basic is life's fragility. So many difficulties can come our way—a storm, car accident, health crisis, loss of a loved one.

Yet there are other threats to our existence as well—loss of meaning, hopelessness, the icy fingers of despair. Such existential anxieties can sap our inner resources, abandoning us to roam in a barren landscape.

When we feel threatened in these ways, we often grope for help and answers. While those who are religious turn to God in such times of crisis, even the most secular amongst us may do the same when we recognise that our situation is beyond human help.

A cry uttered when we feel helpless may float away like the wind when nothing happens to relieve us. But it can also fade like a phantom once the crisis is over and help does come.

We forget the person who helped us when our car broke down along the highway. The surgeon who performed a life-saving operation fades from memory. We forget how our parents cared for and nurtured us through childhood when we become overwhelmed with problems later in life.

And as soon as our difficulties are over, we also quickly forget about any promises to change. The promise, "I will exercise more now that my health scare is over," is soon forgotten once we return to the normal realities of life.

Though promises and commitments made in the heat of crisis can be lasting, they seldom endure because they are pragmatic, utilitarian, and lack reflection. Such promises are prompted by very specific circumstances, and when those circumstances change, the commitments generally fade away.

Ignatian spirituality suggests a helpful "rule" for such circumstances: in times of "desolation," don't make major commitments or promises. In other words, in times of difficulty or despair, don't commit yourself to major changes.

For example, if you are trapped in your car after an accident, don't promise that you will give all your money to the poor if you manage to get out without lifelong injuries.

Rather, we should make important decisions and commitments in places of reflection rather than the heat of the moment. We should not decide to believe in God simply because we walked away from a serious car accident with only a broken arm. Our serious life commitments need to be drawn from much deeper wells in order to be well watered.

LEADERSHIP

a spirituality of service

The leading bird is the first to be shot.

In places where radical egalitarianism is promoted, particularly in the West, the notion of leadership can be problematical. Even when leadership is not an ideological problem, it can be a practical one because it is so challenging to exercise leadership well, and many people have problems with leaders.

Yet leadership is pragmatically necessary in all forms of social life and organisation. Sociologically, it is grounded in the exercise of some form of legitimate authority. Theologically, it is grounded in God's sovereignty and the delegation of that power to humans. The basic implication for both is that the use of power must be accountable.

In the relationship between leader and followers, there is a reciprocal notion of power. One can do what the leader asks, but one can also resist—if one is willing to live with the consequences.

But the exercise of leadership is not easy. The Chinese proverb, "the leading bird is the first to be shot,"[68] expresses clearly the awesome responsibility of leadership.

Two themes that call for further reflection include the way that leadership is exercised and how leaders are perceived by others.

Some leaders are able to motivate and move others in a projected direction through participatory processes, empowerment, and reflection because of their example and wisdom. This does not mean that there will not be opposition and resistance, because there usually is. Rather, such opposition can be negotiated and can deepen the process of change. Change that has gone through purgation is usually more strategic than the change of plain sailing.

However, some leaders are self-serving and misuse their position. When this happens, such leaders reveal themselves as not worthy of their role.

But some leaders are not self-serving, and yet are still judged to be so—a situation suggested by the Chinese proverb. Typically, such leaders are not shot by a distant marksman, but rather by one on their own team.

SET UP FOR A FALL

overextending ourselves

To lift someone over the horse.

The seventeenth-century Dutch proverb, "iemand over het paard tillen,"[69] finds no equivalent in other modern languages. It can be literally translated as "to lift someone *over* the horse"—notice, that it is not to lift someone *on* to the horse.

One meaning implies that a person who is a horse owner is a person of privilege, and so lifting that person up has to do with the person's enhancement or exultation. Thus one who is already privileged is given greater influence and prestige. But to lift that person *over* the horse means that he or she is set up for a fall.[70]

Another related meaning is to lift up a person of low social status to an important societal role. But when the person is unable to cope with this new status, he or she crashes to the ground.

Though more meanings are always possible with proverbs, the core idea is clear. A person is graduated to a role or task for which he or she is unsuited or untrained—and at some point comes crashing down. This idea opens up several important issues.

First and foremost, we are called to be self-aware. It is important for us to know our gifts and abilities and which roles and tasks in life suit us. In light of this self-understanding, we can know when to say "yes" or "no" to opportunities as they present themselves.

Second, it is easy for us to give into the temptation to set unrealistic expectations for ourselves. Thus we become too smart for our own boots. Being unrealistic about high or grandiose demands invites a crash.

Third, one can be deliberately set up by someone else to fail. In the cut-throat world of business or politics, someone might make a pre-emptive strike against an opponent by trying to eliminate that person through self-elimination. One way to do this is by offering a sudden promotion for which the opponent is not ready. In such a scenario, you lift your opponent "*over* the horse," yet your hands remain clean. Though it appears that you have elevated and promoted this person, in actual fact, you have stabbed him or her in the back.

Finally, in good parenting, a "smart aleck" son or daughter may need to be set up for an early fall in order to come to his or her senses.

Both practical wisdom and basic psychology are at play in this interesting proverb.

53

EXPLOITATION

when the well runs dry

The well with sweet water will be exhausted first.

Many of us struggle with the current shortage of political wisdom. Another bewildering aspect of our civil society is the increasing lack of civility. We hear often about workplaces that exercise functional "brutality" in managing their ever-expendable workforce. Such a gloomy picture leads us to wonder what we are doing to each other through our practices of inhumanity!

Yet there are still people around the world who are seeking to do a good job, be respectful to others, work hard, and try to benefit and enhance the organisation or business of which they are a part.

These good people are seldom rewarded, but they are often exploited. The Chinese proverb, "the well with sweet water will be exhausted first,"[71] expresses this reality well.

Hardworking, good-natured, and caring people seldom end up in key positions of power, but their goodness creates a life-giving and hopeful ethos and environment within an organisation. These people create a certain "social capital" in the workplace that is hard to quantify and is often unappreciated by the captains of our outcome-based work practices.

Such people are the oil that keeps the "machine" working well, the humanisers of difficult workplaces.

But because they are under-appreciated and overexploited, the wells from which they draw their sweet water often run dry.

When these good and caring people run dry, they experience a huge personal loss—a loss of self in relation to the very humanity that constitutes their being. "I am no longer myself," they might say. "I can no longer be myself in this place."

Wells run dry when self-care is neglected, and hopes are lost, and dreams are dashed. Someone experiencing such loss might say, "I have given much of myself and there is nothing left to give," or, "I feel ripped off."

Such a scenario invites a setting for recovery so long as the person is able to overcome the inevitable resentment that seeps into an empty well. Recovery calls for stronger self-care, the establishment of boundaries, and space to reflect on important questions, such as "will I leave?" or "if I stay, how can survive better?"

In our pragmatic age, we tend to forget the notion of spirit—not supernatural spiritual forces, but rather a social environment of goodness, joy, respect, cooperation, creativity, justice, and fairness. These things don't appear in a corporation's annual report, but they add spirit and productivity to a workplace.

Bosses and managers who fail to appreciate the importance of these things are foolish, for as the Swedish proverb warns, "when the well is dry, we know it's worth."[72]

<u>54</u>

BACK - TO - FRONT

losing the connection
between means and ends

Putting the cart before the horse.

The Dutch proverb, "het paard achter de wagen spannen,"[73] literally means to harness the horse behind the cart. The self-evident meaning is getting things back-to-front.

This proverb, like so many others, is open to layers of meaning. On the surface, it suggests an act of stupidity—such as putting a cake pan in the oven without any batter. But I wish to make a more ethical reflection about the relationship between ends and means.

Literally, if you want a horse to pull a cart, the horse needs to be harnessed in front of the cart. If you want to bake a cake, you need to make batter. If you want to become wise, you need to learn from your mistakes. If you want to end war, you have to enact peace. More banally, if you want to start your day, you need to get out of bed.

Yet we readily fail to connect ends and means, particularly in our social relationships, because we want quick results at the cost of good processes. We can't have deep friendships without availability and vulnerability. We can't be successful community workers without being consultative. We won't have well-being in our society if justice is downtrodden in our streets.

Oma, who was fond of quoting this proverb, offered a little bit of extra but related advice. In English, it amounted to this: if you want to be a kind person when you grow older, start being kind now. Don't be a miserable and cranky person now—at the age of ten—and think that at fifty you can suddenly decide to be kind. You are putting crankiness first and kindness last. You have the cart before the horse. Let kindness pull you toward the person you wish to become. Good advice!

Gandhi and others have given similar advice. Since a life of goodness is being constantly "pulled" towards goodness, then *be* the person you wish *to become*. And Gandhi issued a related challenge: be the change you wish to see in others and in society.

To put the cart before the horse is not only stupid, but it will also result in stagnation, for there can be no forward movement.

Life is a movement in a certain direction, which requires repetition in order for there to be growth. Whatever direction we might be heading, we need to make sure that the steps we are taking each day are consistent with who we hope to become and what we hope to do.

May each step not only shape our personal well-being, but also involve a commitment to seeking the common good for others.

55

EVIL

the persistence of wrongdoing

Bad weeds never die.

For most of my adult life, I have grown my own vegetables. I love the return cycle of giving food scraps and vegetable trimmings to the chickens and putting sugarcane mulch on the chicken coop floor, which becomes mulch that is worked into my "veggie" gardens, which in turn put beans, peas, tomatoes, celery, cabbage, lettuce, silver beet, and other vegetables on my kitchen table. And of course, there are the fresh eggs.

I don't use pesticides, herbicides, or fertilisers, and I follow companion-planting principles—but weeds never fail to show up in all of my garden beds. Weeding is as much a part of gardening as sowing and harvesting.

Weeding has given me ample time to think about weeds, which are a good metaphor for the undesirable things in our lives and in the world. The Spanish proverb, "Yerba mala nunca muere,"[74] which means bad weeds never die, suggests that we will always need to wrestle with messiness, brokenness, and wrongdoing in our lives and the world.

In considering this analogy, it is helpful to recognise that seedlings and weeds are hard to tell apart at first. So it is with small acts of goodness and tiny misdemeanours. The latter we hardly notice at first, but with time, these misdemeanours can grow into something more sinister and debilitating. Therefore, we need to face such issues earlier rather than later, although postponement always seems to be an attractive option.

When I am unable to attend to my gardens regularly, the weeds always outgrow the vegetables and hinder their growth. Thus we need to be attentive, and we have to deal with the follies and sins in our lives.

It is difficult to come to terms with the persistence of wrongdoing in our lives and the world. Why can't goodness and beauty just flourish? Is the continuation of evil a metaphysical reality? Or is wrongdoing actually a blessing in disguise?

In picking up the last question, I would like to answer it in the affirmative, but in a very qualified way. I do wish that violence and injustice would be banished from our lives and world, but I am not sure what such an ideal world would be like. I have no sense that we would handle such perfection well.

The persistence of evil, on the other hand, saves us from thinking of ourselves as gods and continues to challenge us to seek forgiveness, make reparation, and seek reconciliation. These things are good for us.

Because evil exists in our lives and the world, we need restoration and salvation. It is good for us to live with the sense that we need help and we need to improve.

But having said all of that, I wish that goodness would prevail!

56

JUSTICE

the fading hope of the poor

*Laws are like cobwebs: where the small flies are caught,
and the great [creatures] break through.*[75]

Most people have a good sense of fairness—particularly when their own
sense of what is just and fair is violated in some way. The issue need not
be big, for it may be something simple, such as not being credited for work
well done while others are praised and thanked.

Though we may react when we think we have been treated unfairly,
we don't necessarily extend that degree of fairness to our relationships
with others. Most often, we are not that generous!

But we should all be concerned about how goodness and justice are distributed within our body politic. Despite legislation about equal rights and laws against discrimination, justice is often perceived as preferential treatment.

Social stratification has intensified in our world, and many people who used to be in the middle class find themselves slipping down the ladder. Racism is not only alive and well but is experiencing a resurgence. Discrimination is being flaunted during a time when millions of displaced people are seeking a new home.

In a world increasingly marked by fear and national self-interest, the arteries of social goodness seem to be hardening, and self-justification and other-disregarding is emerging as the new logic of the body politic.

In this setting, the old English proverb, "Laws are like cobwebs: where the small flies are caught, and the great [creatures] break through," is becoming even more relevant.

Those who are "outsiders" in our social landscape are, generally speaking, the "little people." Unto them, we happily apply the full brunt of the law. With the drastic reduction in voluntary legal services, we are quite happy to see them locked away safely in our prisons.

But the "big players" in our society can easily avoid legal charges—for corporate tax evasion, money laundering, shonky business practices—by hiring a gaggle of the best lawyers in town. Such schemes are forms of collusion that enable those with means and influence to gain advantage in spite of illegal practices.

In the Judeo-Christian tradition as well as other religions, there is a serious and oft-repeated theme regarding justice and care for the poor. To cite one text, which identifies the king in ancient Israel as the bearer of justice: "Give the king your justice, O God. . . may he judge your people with righteousness and your poor with justice" (Psalm 72: 1–2). The psalmist continues, "For he delivers the needy when they call, the poor and those who have no helper. He has pity on the weak and needy, and saves the lives of the needy" (72: 12–13).

When goodness and compassion shrivel in the body politic, justice becomes the privilege of the powerful and the fading hope of the poor. In this we not only harm others, but we also diminish ourselves!

57

PASSION

counterbalancing stagnation
and blind enthusiasm

If the stove is hot, even wet firewood will burn.

There is a strange and questionable idea afoot in the modern world, which is that we should live balanced lives, and when our life is in balance, we will experience wholeness and well-being.

I would like us to rethink this idea. First of all, it is doubtful whether wholeness comes from balance. Rather, our sense of well-being comes from tension, suffering, and transformation, which make way for new integration and growth.

Second, while the notion of balance sounds attractive, it can easily lead to stagnation. For balance is about maintaining equilibrium, whereas growth emerges in the dialectic between various creative tensions.

Thus it is far better to be passionate than balanced. The former promises forward movement, whereas the latter suggests the status quo.

The Chinese proverb, "if the stove is hot, even wet firewood will burn,"[76] suggests that the fires of passion can contain so much energy that even a "wet blanket" (i.e., negative opposition) cannot snuff them out.

However, we do need to consider how passion might run opposite to the "danger" of being balanced. Obviously, while we can be overly cautious in seeking balance, our passion can drive us towards blind enthusiasm.

This raises a much more interesting series of questions about how balance can become more dynamic and how passion can be harnessed. Does passion need to be revolutionary, or can it be expressed as a careful gradualism? Does a life in balance need its boundaries to be expanded in order to remain healthy? These two dynamics seem to need one another in counter-balancing ways.

The key problem with passion is overreaching. Passion can have an almost godlike quality, where someone is deeply moved about an issue or concern and becomes galvanised to spring into action. The problem is not passion, but the move "to spring" into action, which can be premature, impulsive, and inherently unrealistic.

But to have a strong emotion and desire to do something is better than living in the quagmire of indifference and passivity. So how does one channel passion?

First, passion needs reflection. Second, passion needs consultation. Third, passion needs appropriate timing.

With these in place, passion needs courage and the willingness to suffer—even in defeat. There are no guarantees that what we do will win the day, for too much wet wood can snuff out a fire.

58

PREOCCUPATION

a failure in relevance

*The village is burning and the village prostitute
is washing her hair.*

One doesn't need to be a great student of history to realise that people can be blind to the momentous things that are happening around them. In the past, people were insufficiently aware of the nature and implications of the industrial revolution. In the present, we are insufficiently aware of the long-term implications of climate change and the creation of techno-humanoids, where technology and biology fuse into a "new" creation.

We readily shake our heads as we condemn our forebears for the stupid mistakes they made in the colonial period, or those who lived in the twentieth century of Stalin's communism and Hitler's Nazism. But in our own time, we fail to see the many challenges confronting us. The Greek proverb, "the village is burning and the village prostitute is washing her hair,"[77] is an appropriate wake-up call.

This proverb evokes rather ludicrous contrasting pictures. There is a fire in town, and this person is wasting water washing her hair; disaster is everywhere, and she continues her mundane routine. And the water should have been used to help put out the fire!

We could try to rationalise this scene. As a person on the margins of the community, the woman might be thinking that with her tarnished reputation, there is nothing worth saving in this village. As an outsider, she might be assuming that her help would not be appreciated anyway.

But such speculation is beside the point. The fundamental meaning is that when we become preoccupied with ordinary life, we can become blind to the bigger issues of our community or world.

At this point in the twenty-first century, we can see the unfolding of Michel Foucault's concern regarding the nexus between knowledge and power. His point is that knowledge is power, which involves both the politics of secrecy and propaganda.

In the Western world, Foucault's warning is becoming apparent in the way that truth is the casualty of the loudest and most powerful voices. Truth is stumbling in the street, so that we no longer have sufficient common ground under our feet in order to have a dialogue or a debate. We only have verbal slinging matches and the work of "trolls" to reinforce propaganda and intimidate opponents.

Consequently, more than a village is burning down. Our whole socio-political fabric is being incinerated. Yet we continue to consume our daily ritual of lattes to give some normality to our lives!

Nero, so we are told, fiddled while Rome burned. What instruments are in our hands instead of the buckets of water that we should be carrying?

59
=====

WORSHIPFUL

a spirituality of adoration

In childhood you are playful, in youth you are lustful,
[and] in old age you are feeble.
So when will you, before God, be worshipful?[78]

This Afghan proverb spans the whole of human life and touches on some core themes. The question it raises, "when will you, before God, be worshipful?" can easily be misconstrued, for we might readily assume that the time for faith, prayer, and worship is in our latter years, when fragility knocks at our door. Such a misunderstanding suggests that sheer helplessness is the only precondition for spirituality.

This proverb might also suggest that we will only be worshipful in the afterlife. Another interpretation can be summed up in the word "never." Within the cycles of life's playfulness, lustfulness, and feebleness, there is no room for worship at all.

Yet I would like to suggest that we are called to be worshipful in every phase of our existence.

In childhood, we can be enamoured with the beauty and power of nature and the care of our parents and other figures, thereby living with a sense of wonder that emerges in worship and gratitude. We can also be struck by our smallness and vulnerability and so we worship the Creator God, whose greatness and protective strength fills us with awe. Feebleness is not the sole domain of the elderly.

In youth and beyond, as we assert ourselves and follow our passions, we remain vulnerable. For we often feel distressed and fragile because of the power of our emotions and the stirrings of our inner being as they seek to dominate and determine our very existence. Here, again, worship can be a healing deterrent as we turn to the Redeemer God for healing and renewal and to gain an inner direction that is formed by our values and not simply our unbridled desires.

Old age ushers in a time of grateful remembrance, where our worship becomes a song to the God of faithfulness amidst our precarious journeys.

Thus worship is appropriate for every phase of life and is intrinsic to the human condition. The issue is not whether we worship, but *who* or *what* we worship.

Here the challenge of discernment comes into play. It is easy to worship the creation or the creature and not the Creator. It is easy to rely on ourselves and not the renewing and empowering Spirit. It is easy to focus on the gift and lose sight of the giver.

When we worship, we give praise to the One who is worthy of our gratitude. While we should be thankful to others and for all that is good in the human community, worship is for God alone. In worship, we properly situate ourselves. We are not the gods of this world, but are creatures made in God's image, who are called to worship God and serve others.

60

SINGULAR SOLUTIONS

blinkered to complexity

If your only tool is a hammer, you will see every problem as a nail.

At this point in the twenty-first century, despite hoped-for changes in the so-called Arab Spring and our ability to mobilise people through the use of social media, we feel increasingly disempowered to bring about change for the common good.

The German social philosopher Jürgen Habermas observes that because we come from increasingly fragile and often dysfunctional families, we lack the resilience to stand up to the larger configurations of power in our world. Thus he calls us to construct intermediate associations that can become communities of resistance.

But whether we are on our own as isolated individuals or part of small communities, we run the risk of misunderstanding the complexities of our global world. As such, we make trite and often ineffectual suggestions about how to change some aspects of our society.

The African Ambede proverb, "if your only tool is a hammer, you will see every problem as a nail,"[79] hits the nail on the head. From a small space in a complex world, we tend to come up with small solutions that are really not solutions at all.

The more embattled and marginalised a group or community is within the broader society, the more bizarre their hoped-for dreams for change become, for a limited horizon fosters a limited vision, which in turn produces singular and unhelpful solutions.

For example, many Christian groups in the Western world now feel marginalised by mainstream society, which used to be predominately Christian. These groups are suggesting that a return to the Christendom of the past will both save the church and society.

This longing for the past has become a hammer in their hands. The more this longing gets frustrated, the more they become blind to other possible solutions. They also become more willing to use coercion to bring about this hoped-for solution. Coercion has been part of the church's long march throughout history, and the more recent attempts at regime change in Iraq and Afghanistan included Christian impulses.

One way forward is to consider what we do not have rather than focusing on the hammer in our hands. Maybe it's time to consider the empty hand, the dark night, the desert place.

Perhaps the renewal of the church and society through the recovery of its humanity, care, community, the common good, and the reign of peace needs to go through the eye of the needle. In the place of purgation, the prayers of lament, the cry of the wounded heart, and a *theologia crucis* (theology of the cross), the salvation of the world may spring forth like flowers in the desert.

The hammer will not do, for the nail is not the problem. Nor will the sword provide the answer.

For we have all lost our way. We have become the gods of the modern world. Our godlikeness has stripped away our humanity, which is held in broken hearts and hands.

We need the healing of the desert, darkness, and emptiness before we can learn to use the instruments of restoration.

61

UNADVENTUROUS

living in a bubble

Old ships remain on land.

While some might say that there is a hero in all of us, we must admit that there is also a coward in each of us. Though we may be committed to adventure, we are also concerned with safety.

This concern increases as we age, and we tend to become much more careful and less adventurous as time goes on, possibly even more fearful.

The old Dutch proverb, "oude schepen blijven aan land," can be translated as "old ships remain on land." The German variant, "teure Schiffe bleiben am Rande,"[80] means "expensive ships stay on land," and it used to be disparagingly applied to older and demanding spinsters who remained unmarried in the family home. But this proverb can be applied in more general ways.

We can readily become stuck in the circumstances of life by failing to take risks, being fearful, and being unreasonable in our demands and expectations. Our basic need for safety and security can easily lock us in so that we don't venture into the fray of life.

By nature, some people simply prefer the closet, where they won't be noticed, to taking centre stage in the arena, where they might face failure.

Those who have taken risks and been battered and bruised in the process may decide never to risk again.

But the thrust of this proverb is that ships are built for the sea and are not meant to remain on land. As humans, are we meant for the waves rather than the safety of the shore?

How we respond to this question has to do with our growth and development. If we want to expand rather than narrow ourselves and our horizons, then we need to venture forth into life.

But something needs to call us forward from our present situation. To put this more strongly, we need to be lured out of our securities.

I suggest two fundamental motivations: either a greater love or a divine invitation or calling may call us forward. Both are powerful enough to dislodge us and put us out to sea.

Yet a hard, less travelled road may also propel us forward—when the ground collapses under our feet, and we have to jump into the unknown unprepared.

Though it is better to take risks made by choice rather than those made by external factors, there is always the possibility of happy sailing, even when old age beckons!

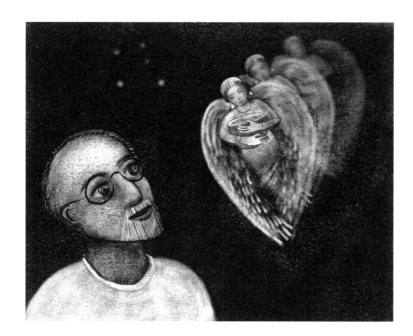

62

TO PAUSE

the gentle art of disengagement

There was a pause—
just long enough for an angel to pass, flying slowly.[81]

At this point in the twenty-first century, despite our progress and economic enhancement, our lives tend to feel harassed. Busy, distracted, and uncertain about the sustainability of our world, we are internally displaced and fragmented. An inner peace eludes us, and joy seems to have forsaken us.

In these circumstances, we should not be surprised that many people, while alienated from the major religions of our time, are nurturing a spiritual quest for inner equilibrium.

Thus we hear many voices recommending that we disengage from our communication devices from time to time. People talk about mindfulness, reflection, and meditation. Some suggest that we need to take time just to "stare out of the window."

This is a healthy and small, but significant, expression of self-care that can help us recover from the intensity of our work environments and from the busyness of our urban lifestyle.

But we need to make sure that we don't drag the *modus operandi* of our daily busyness into being busy with our meditation and other spiritual practices. We need to recognise how difficult it is for us to "down tools" and learn the art of silence and solitude.

The early twentieth-century novelist Ronald Firbank points us in the right direction with this quotation. We need to discover the gentle art of disengagement in order to lay down our preoccupations and compulsions. As we do, we are tackling one of the citadels of our modern age, which makes us feel that we must constantly make things happen because no one else will do that for us. In other words, we must expose the modern myth of the self-made human being who alone must carry the responsibility for his or her life and world.

In such a construction, there is no leisure, no downtime, no Sabbath, no grace, no beauty, no gift or goodness that comes our way.

The practice of solitude helps us to receive the *gift* of inhabiting a place of openness and emptiness, where surprises may come.

Who knows what that surprise may be? A caress for a bruised heart. A gentle inner encouragement in places of despair. A new insight. A potential new direction. A correction. A reminder. A whisper from the edge of eternity.

63

DEFLECTION

the blame game

Some people do not blame the shortness of their own rope,
but rather blame the deepness of the old well.[82]

Many people feel the precarious nature of our present-day existence. Our world feels less safe and life feels less certain. We want to trust that our governments and social institutions will do the right thing for all of us, but we are no longer sure. Even the family as a place of security seems much more fragile. The elderly are more likely to be put away somewhere in an aged-care facility than to be cared for in their familiar surroundings.

With uncertainty and insecurity comes the blame game. While we may blame ourselves for the state of the world, or the nature of our government, or the dynamics of our family, we are much more likely to blame others for their lack of attention or care.

If we can identify someone who has failed us, we can deflect responsibility from ourselves. But this will hardly make us feel any better or safer. In fact, it may make us feel worse, for anger and resentment tend to follow in the wake of blame.

Having said this, I am not implying that other people always do the right thing, for this is certainly not the case. Others sin against us and wound us, and it is good to call people on this.

Though we should not be the dumping ground for other people's "madness," blaming them will not get us very far on the road to recovery. Somewhere, justice, forgiveness, or reconciliation will have to come in view.

But when we broaden the dynamic of blame beyond the personal and apply to it to the government, or major institutions, or the age in which we are living, or God, we are entering rather difficult territory. For there is no sure ground under our feet, and we can easily end up in the "swamp" of despair or self-pity.

One way to avoid this terrain is to rethink one of the major propositions of our age: the matter of entitlement, which has been sculpted in our inner being through the daily mantra that we can be anything, do anything, have anything, and that our rights will guarantee a good life.

What a myth! What propaganda! What nonsense! Life is precarious. Unexpected things happen. Things don't always work out. We make mistakes, and so do others. The stock market can crash. A cyclone or typhoon can cause great damage. We may lose a job. Our marriage may fail. We will have health issues in later life, unless we die of an unexpected heart attack early in life.

Yes, we can blame others, God, or the government. But we would do better to embrace the notion that life is not a picnic. It has both mountaintop experiences as well as deep valleys.

64

AN ORDINARY LIFE

an extraordinary commitment
to the common good

*The highest art is the art of living an ordinary life
in an extraordinary manner.*[83]

In traditional societies, one is dedicated to living an ordinary life—and the more ordinary the better—because life is not about outstanding individuals, but the community as whole.

In our twenty-first-century world, the fundamental orientation is the significance of the individual. Our primary commitment is not the betterment of society, but our individual growth and enhancement.

This focus has major implications for our sense of loyalty to our country, the institutions we are part of, and our family. Yet many of us feel we can no longer trust the government; we are increasingly fickle about our loyalty to institutions; and the family has become a weakened "institution" in the modern world.

In light of this, how are we to understand the ancient Tibetan proverb, "The highest art is the art of living an ordinary life in an extraordinary manner"? What is an ordinary life? What does it look like to live this life in an extraordinary way?

Despite our present-day fears about being ordinary, in the Tibetan sense, being ordinary is neither colourless nor meaningless. Rather, it is full of the richness of traditions, sparkles with natural beauty, celebrates community, and is impregnated with a deep spirituality. There is nothing flat, mundane, or boring about such a life.

To live an ordinary life in an extraordinary way suggests that we internalise the values of joy and commitment rather than assume them as part of our socialisation. Thus we live a communal identity with personal conviction. We understand, reinforce, and share the richness of our tradition and spirituality.

The monks of the medieval Christian world understood this well. Amidst a darkened Europe, the Benedictine monasteries became pockets of hope by forging a way of life and a spirituality with a similar mantra: to live the ordinary in an extraordinary way.

The Benedictine monks lived these values with personal conviction in the service of others. But they also believed that the ordinary was itself extraordinary.

In Benedictine spirituality, to serve the neighbour is to serve God, and to live in community in the present is to anticipate the grand banquet of the life to come. In the daily affairs of life, God is as much present and pleased with our work as with the worship and art in a monastery's chapel. Washing pots and pans is as important as cleansing our soul from persistent pollution.

The true saints of our world are not those who pontificate from mountaintops, but rather those who wash dishes, give love, share resources, build relationships, commit themselves to the common good, and wash the feet of the world. This is basic. This is ordinary. This is extraordinary.

65

INQUISITIVENESS

an ongoing quest for wisdom

If I know I will die tomorrow,
I can still learn something tonight.[84]

There is something wonderful about being inquisitive. While the ongoing quest for knowledge can become a power trip, the longing for wisdom can become a beautiful desire to understand and serve others and to make the world a better place.

Yet this noble quest can begin to wane for many reasons. The longing for understanding has limits, and being wise does not necessarily make us happy.

With aging, longings may shrink, curiosity may weaken, and we may begin to close down our inner questing.

The ancient Tibetan proverb, "if I know I will die tomorrow, I can still learn something today," suggests that we should never close down the arteries of our curiosity because life is an ongoing learning process. We can continue to hope that even when we stand at the portal of death, we might still gain further insights.

Thus we are woven into a web of mutuality. This is both wonderful and challenging!

It is tragic, however, when this web of giving and receiving is fractured, as when exploitation becomes our *modus operandi.*

Therefore, though our needs and responses to needs have become commercialised and monetarised, we must not lose the "milk" of human kindness in these social arrangements.

One of the highlights of my life was the care I received from the oncology staff, particularly the nurses, during my year of chemotherapy in a public hospital. Though they were all doing their job and following their chosen career path, for which they received reasonable (but not enough) pay, their attentiveness and loving care made such a difference. I continue to be grateful, even so many years later.

One person's needs can be another's employment, but this should never be the whole story. We enhance our own humanity when we care for those in need or when we show love and compassion. When we take those values and dynamics out of the equation, we diminish others and especially ourselves.

Though economics and mechanistic arrangements are necessary, they are not the whole story. The "milk" of human kindness will do more to nurture us than all the mechanistic arrangements in the world.

SILENCE

the gift of solitude

From the tree of silence hangs the fruit of tranquillity.[89]

In our busy world and lifestyles, we can become truly lost. With the on-going pressure to reinvent ourselves and our careers, we cannot be at rest for even a moment—especially if we need constant connection with the virtual world.

Internally fraught, fractured, and busy, we continue to externalise ourselves in the hope that we will be heard and seen as significant. Yet this sense of significance is not internally generated, but is only a social construction. How poor we are if our whole being is defined by the accumulation of quick Instagrams from others!

Living this way is a zero game. For if our identity is embedded in others' approval, it will never be enough.

It is time for us to go inward, just as one turns homeward to a fireplace and warmth in winter. We need to find solace within our inner selves. We need to become more centred and reflective so that we can garner the fruits of solitude.

In a world of doing, we need to recover our own being. We need to live more securely in our own skin and learn to listen to our own heartbeat and the movement of goodness and creativity in our lives.

While the "world" of silence and solitude may seem strange, we need to enter this territory if we wish to find ourselves. Lost in our much-doing, the quiet road of retrieval must become a road that is more travelled.

Among the Desert Fathers and Mothers as well as the monastic tradition of Christianity and virtually all other religious traditions, the practices of withdrawal, solitude, and contemplation were intrinsic to spiritual growth and well-being.

In a world that shouts at us with multiple voices, we need to find an inner solace, where we can begin to find our own voice.

But before we can discern this, we need to find our own "heart," the inner longings and desires that transcend the anorexic mantras of contemporary society.

To hear anew, we need to be still enough to listen. To listen well, we need to give ourselves the gift of time and a lonely place. We must not be afraid of what we hear, but we do need to be discerning. Then we need to have the courage to live out what we discern.

Index:
Proverbs and Sayings

Good water even if made murky will become clear again after the dirt
    has settled., 12

He [she] that touches pitch shall be defiled., 56

If I know I will die tomorrow, I can still learn something tonight., 130

If the rat cannot flee, let it make way for the tortoise., 44

If the stove is hot, even wet firewood will burn., 114

If the Tao or Buddha rises one foot, the demon rises ten., 76

If your only tool is a hammer, you will see every problem as a nail., 120

In a good book the best is between the lines., 80

In childhood you are playful, in youth you are lustful, [and] in old age
    you are feeble. So when will you, before God, be worshipful? , 118

In for a penny, in for a pound., 4

It is better to fix what you have, than wait to get what you don't have., 38

It is not with the first stroke that the tree falls., 54

Laws are like cobwebs: where the small flies are caught, and the great
    [creatures] break through., 112

Love laughs at locksmiths., 30

Most of us trouble others, but few like to trouble themselves., 86

No evil without its advantages., 50

No one knows where the shoe pinches as well as the one who wears it., 10

Not all chefs carry their special knives., 26

Not every flower can be a rose., 36

Nothing can get into a closed fist, 74

Old ships remain on land., 122

One can cut large thongs from another person's leather., 42

One man's death is another man's income., 138

One man [woman] who's been flogged is worth two who haven't., 62

One's illness can be cured, but one's fate cannot., 84

Peace is not the absence of war, it is a virtue, a state of mind, a
    disposition of benevolence, confidence and justice., 68

People are blind in their own cause., 22

Putting the cart before the horse., 108

Shared sorrow is half the grief., 14

Some people do not blame the shortness of their own rope, but rather
    blame the deepness of the old well., 126

Staying means attachment., 94

The cow of another always has a bigger udder., 78

The danger past, God is forgotten., 100

The day is short and the work is long., 134

The frog does not drink up the pond in which it lives., 28

The highest art is the art of living an ordinary life in an extraordinary manner., 128

The leading bird is the first to be shot., 102

The most potent weapon in the hand of the oppressor is the mind of the oppressed., 92

The one who gives to another bestows on oneself., 70

The one who swallows 'udala' (apple) seed must consider the size of one's anus., 40

The reed before the wind lives on, while mighty oaks do fall., 82

There was a pause—just long enough for an angel to pass, flying slowly., 124

The village is burning and the village prostitute is washing her hair., 116

The well with sweet water will be exhausted first., 106

To add water to wine., 52

To drag solutions out of nowhere., 72

To kick against the pricks., 32

To lift someone over the horse., 104

To put a stick in the wheel., 34

To sugar the pill., 58

To waste a candle to find a flea., 20

Water thirty-three feet deep is easily measured, but a person's thoughts are hard to fathom., 8

Where there is desire, there is ability., 60

Women hold up half the sky., 98

Topical Index

Endnotes

1   J. Speake, ed., *The Oxford Dictionary of Proverbs* (Oxford: Oxford University Press, 2004), 259.

2   Dutch for "grandmother."

3   If the proverb is published elsewhere, I will reference that as well.

4   F. A. Stoett, *Nederlandse Spreekwoorden en Gezegden* (Zutphen: B.V. W. J. Thieme & Chie, 1981).

5   Stoett, *Nederlandse Spreekwoorden*, 76.

6   Stoett, *Nederlandse Spreekwoorden*, 76.

7   Stoett, *Nederlaandse Spreekwoorden*, 206.

8   Stoett, *Nederlaandse Spreekwoorden*, 206.

9   C. Skillen, *Russian Proverbs* (Belfast: The Appletree Press, Ltd., 1994), 37.

10   J. Simpson, *The Concise Oxford Dictionary of Proverbs* (Oxford: Oxford University Press, 1985), 120.

11   Oma's "Little Red Book."

12   J. S. Rohsenow, *ABC Dictionary of Chinese Proverbs* (Richmond, UK: Curzon, 2002), 139.

13   Stoett, *Nederlandse Spreekworden*, 282–83.

14   D. L. Eugenio, ed., *Philippine Folk Literature: The Proverbs,* vol. 6 (Quezon City: University of the Philippines Press, 2002), 381.

15   Stoett, *Nederlandse Spreekworden*, 103.

16   E. van Eeden, ed., *Groot spreekwoordenboek* (Aartselaar, Belgium: Zuidnederlandse Uitgeverij, 1997), 19.

17   www.homeinsteaders.org/authors/native-american-proverbs/#sthash.DGllgsc.Z.dpbs

18   G. L. Apperson, *The Wordsworth Dictionary of Proverbs* (Ware, UK: Wordsworth Reference, 1993), 79.

19   Apperson, *The Wordsworth Dictionary of Proverbs*, 54–55.

20   https://blog.udemy.com/arabic-proverbs/

21   Stoett, *Nederlandse Spreekworden*, 179.

22   www.homeinsteaders.org/authors/native-american-proberbs/#sthash.DGllgsc.Z.dpbs

23   Apperson, *The Wordsworth Dictionary of Proverbs*, 385.

24   Stoett, *Nederlandse Spreekworden*, 334.

25   Stoett, *Nederlandse Spreekworden*, 295.

26   Oma's "Little Red Book."

27   https://blog.udemy.com/arabic-proverbs/

28   https://hubpages.com/literature/50-Most-Important-African-Proverbs-and-their-meanings-words-of-our-elders

29   Stoett, *Nederlandse Spreekworden*, 271.

30   https://hubpages.com/literature/50-Most-Important-African-Proverbs-and-their-meanings-words-of-our-elders

31   Skillen, *Russian Proverbs*, 24.

32   Rohsenow, *ABC Dictionary of Chinese Proverbs*, 29.

33   Stoett, *Nederlandse Spreekworden*, 191.

34   Apperson, *The Wordsworth Dictionary of Proverbs*, 194.

35   Speake, *Oxford Dictionary of Proverbs*, 98.

36   Oma's "Little Red Book."

37   www.hp.europe.de/kd-europtravel/gaelic/proverb/htm

38   Stoett, *Nederlandse Spreekworden*, 251.

39   Stoett, *Nederlandse Spreekworden*, 254.

40   www.fluentu.com/spanish/blog/spanish-proverbs/

41   Skillen, *Russian Proverbs*, 56.

42   Apperson, *The Wordsworth Dictionary of Proverbs*, 155.

43   Apperson, *The Wordsworth Dictionary of Proverbs*, 247.

44   Rohsenow, *ABC Dictionary of Chinese Proverbs*, 113.

45   N. Rees, *Brewer's Famous Quotations* (London: Weidenfeld & Nicolson, 2006), 439.

46   Apperson, *The Wordsworth Dictionary of Proverbs*, 247.

47   Speake, *The Oxford Dictionary of Proverbs*, 153.

48   Stoett, *Nederlandse Spreekworden*, 117.

49   www.hp.europe.de/kd-europtravel/gaelic/proverb.htm

50   Rohsenow, *ABC Dictionary of Chinese Proverbs*, 29.

51   Oaks.nvg.org/Swedish-proverbs.html

52   Apperson, *The Wordsworth Dictionary of Proverbs*, 185.

53   Oaks.nvg.org/swedish-proverbs.html

54   Speake, *Oxford Dictionary of Proverbs*, 183.

55 Rohsenow, *ABC Dictionary of Chinese Proverbs*, 194.

56 Eugenio, ed., *Philippine Folk Literature*, 581.

57 Oma's "Little Red Book."

58 Apperson, *The Wordsworth Dictionary of Proverbs*, 607.

59 Stoett, *Nederlandse Spreekworden*, 177–178.

60 Speake, *Oxford Dictionary of Proverbs*, 103.

61 S. Ratcliffe, ed., *The Oxford Dictionary of Thematic Quotations* (Oxford: Oxford University Press, 2000), 366.

62 Stoett, *Nederlandse Spreekworden*, 54

63 Apperson, *The Wordsworth Dictionary of Proverbs*, 537

64 Speake, *Oxford Dictionary of Proverbs*, 89.

65 Speake, *Oxford Dictionary of Proverbs*, 89.

66 Rohsenow, *ABC Dictionary of Chinese Proverbs*, 41.

67 Apperson, *The Wordsworth Dictionary of Proverbs*, 135.

68 Rosenow, *ABC Dictionary of Chinese Proverbs*, 104.

69 Oma's "Little Red Book."

70 Stoett, *Nederlandse Spreekworden*, 247.

71 Rosenow, *ABC Dictionary of Chinese Proverbs*, 42.

72 oaks.nvg.org/swedish-proverbs.html

73 Oma's "Little Red Book."

74 www.fluenta.com/blog/spanish/spanish proverbs/

75 Apperson, *The Wordsworth Dictionary of Proverbs*, 353.

76 Rohsenow, *ABC Dictionary of Chinese Proverbs*, 124.

77 www.geocities.jp/nomonomogreek/Proverbs/Proverbs.htm

78 www.inspirationalstories.com/proverbs/t/afghan

79 https://matadornetwork.com/bnt/50-african-proverbs-to-get-you-thinking/

80 Stoett, *Nederlandse Spreekworden*, 279.

81 R. Firbank quoted in S. Ratcliffe, ed., *The Oxford Dictionary of Thematic Quotations*, 402.

82 Rohsenow, *ABC Dictionary of Chinese Proverbs*, 8.

83 https://www.scoopwhoop.com/28-Soul-Stirring-Tibetan-Proverbs/#.3q3hhsbuf

84 https://www.scoopwhoop.com/28-Soul-Stirring-Tibetan-Proverbs/#.3q3hhsbuf

85 https://matadornetwork.com/bnt/50-african-proverbs-to-get-you-thinking/

86 Apperson, *The Wordsworth Dictionary of Proverbs*, 136.

87 www.geocities.jp/nomonomogreek/Proverbs/Proverbs.htm

88 Stoett, *Nederlandse Spreekworden*, 80.

89 proverbials.com/peruvian-proverbs/

By the Same Author

The Art of Healing Prayer

Catch the Wind: church where people matter

Cry Freedom: with voices from the third world

Dare to Journey with Henri Nouwen

Finding Naasicaa: Letters of Hope in an Age of Anxiety

Hear the Ancient Wisdom: A Meditational Reader for the Whole Year
from the Early Church Fathers up to the Pre-Reformation

Hear the Heart Beat with Henri Nouwen

In the Footsteps of an Ancient Faith

Let My People Go with Martin Luther King Jr.

Life in Full Stride: Faith-Stretching Reflections for Christians in the
Real World

Of Martyrs, Monks and Mystics

Ragged Edges: poems from the margins

Resist the Powers with Jacques Ellul

Sabbath Time

Seek the Silences with Thomas Merton

Seize the Day with Dietrich Bonhoeffer

Wash the Feet of the World with Mother Teresa

Whispers from the Edge of Eternity:
Reflections on Life and Faith in a Precarious World

Lightning Source UK Ltd.
Milton Keynes UK
UKHW05f0451020918
328162UK00007B/40/P

9 781909 281592